# Without Ritalin

## A Natural Approach to ADD

## Samuel A. Berne, O.D., F.C.O.V.D.

### Keats Publishing

Chicago   New York   San Francisco   Lisbon   London   Madrid   Mexico City
Milan   New Delhi   San Juan   Seoul   Singapore   Sydney   Toronto

**Library of Congress Cataloging-in-Publication Data**

Berne, Samuel A.
    Without ritalin : a natural approach to ADD / Samuel A. Berne.
       p.    cm.
    Includes bibliographical references and index.
    ISBN 0-658-01215-0 (alk. paper)
      1.  Attention-deficit hyperactivity disorder—Alternative treatment.
2.  Attention-deficit disorder in children—Alternative treatment.    3.  Holistic
medicine.    I.  Title.

RJ506.H9  B47    2001
616.85'89—dc21                         2001029548

## Keats Publishing

A Division of The McGraw·Hill Companies

2  3  4  5  6  7  8  9  0   DOC/DOC   0  9  8  7  6  5  4  3  2

ISBN 0-658-01215-0

This book was set in Berkeley
Printed and bound by R. R. Donnelley—Crawfordsville

Cover design by Anne LoCascio

This book is printed on acid-free paper.

*I would like to thank my wife Charly*
*who inspires me every day*
*to be a better person.*

# Contents

# Preface

After writing my first book, *Creating Your Personal Vision: A Mind-Body Guide for Better Eyesight* in 1994, I decided not to write any more books. It took too much time and energy. Well, sometimes what we think we are supposed to do is not always the case.

I began treating adults and children fifteen years ago while studying and working at the Gesell Institute, a multidisciplinary clinic devoted to assisting people with learning and developmental problems. Although the term *ADD* (Attention Deficit Disorder) was not yet coined, every person we worked with had difficulty focusing and concentrating. As my own personal development evolved, taking many twists and turns as life usually does, a group of mentors helped guide my career. The oldest among them, Dr. Hazel Parcells, was an active 103-year-old chiropractor and naturopath with whom I studied until she died at the age of 106. Dr. Parcells taught me a great deal about health and wellness. She used to say that in our work we are cleaning up the inner environment of our patient's bodies so that disharmony cannot exist there.

Two years ago when I started writing this book, I really did not know where it would take me. But there was one thing I knew for sure. Thus, it is with humility and grace that I welcome the adults and children who come into my office every day in search of answers, for they continually teach me how to work with this growing problem of Attention Deficit Hyperactivity Disorder (AD/HD).

I hope this book gives you a new direction for seeking help and as a self-healing guide. There are no easy answers, but if you make a little progress every day you are on the right path. Keep asking for guidance and help. Remember, healing is an upward spiraling process.

# Introduction

Vincent was in grade school and apparently hating it. His parents, teachers, and counselors had no doubt that he was highly intelligent but observed that he did not conform. He couldn't sit at his desk without wriggling. He had difficulty reading, writing, and taking tests. He didn't seem able to follow directions or complete his homework. He preferred to draw his rather bizarre pictures. Also, Vincent sometimes made inappropriate noises and gestures in the classroom. He asked a lot of questions and was thought to be a disruptive influence. He had too much energy and just didn't fit in.

At a parent-teacher conference, Vincent's teacher asked, "Have you thought of putting Vincent on Ritalin?" His parents soon found themselves in a psychiatrist's office, where Vincent was diagnosed with ADD (Attention Deficit Disorder). The drug of choice, Ritalin, was prescribed for him.

Ritalin made Vincent quiet and subdued. He lost his manic edge. If he drew at all, his drawings were rather dull. He didn't appear to be as intelligent, inquisitive, or demanding, but his parents, teachers, and counselors agreed that it was a small price to pay for peace in the classroom. In short, Vincent became another unremarkable, average, docile child. Imagine what the world would have lost if Vincent's last name were Van Gogh.

I'm not suggesting that Vincent Van Gogh suffered from ADD (although, by all accounts, he might have). Nor am I suggesting that every child who has ADD is necessarily a genius. The point is that families, schools, and institutions (even society at large) are increasingly intolerant of people who don't fit in—particularly within our schools and day-care systems. If we drug or otherwise coerce these children into conformity, how will our Albert Einsteins, our Pablo Picassos, our Wolfgang Mozarts, our Rosa Parkses, or our Stephen Hawkings emerge? Study the biographies of any number of extraordinary figures, both historical and contemporary, and an over-whelming number of them reveal some sort of childhood "pathologies" that, by today's standards and practices, warrant diagnosis and drug treatment.

My fear is that the currently favored drug therapies for ADD are stamping out the "different" kids, many of whom may develop into adults who push the envelope. Society as a whole, with all its wonderful diversity, will suffer.

If that big picture doesn't move you, consider this: The drug therapies extensively promoted by pharmaceutical corporations and their clients, the medical profession, have been proven beyond all doubt to be damaging and toxic. If there were no alternatives, perhaps we would be prepared to pay the enormous price drug therapies cost our society and the health of the individuals within it. But there are alternatives. That's why I've written this book.

Why should you believe me? In my private practice of behavioral optometry, I specialize in the treatment of adults and children with various learning/developmental, reading, and attention problems. While attending the Gesell Institute of Infant/Child Development, I learned the importance of working with children and adults in a multidisciplinary setting. I am also a founding member of the Parcells

Center for Personal Transformation, which is dedicated to disseminating information on the principles of naturopathic medicine and nutrition.

On the face of it, optometry and vision therapy may seem to be an unlikely route to a specialty in ADD. But when you consider that vision is both a primary key to, and a valuable indicator of, a child's development, then it may be easier to understand how I became interested in ADD. Behavioral "problems" frequently reflect developmental problems in the brain and nervous system. The development of the brain and the development of vision are intimately linked.

Researchers are now connecting certain vision problems with ADD and AD/HD (Attention Deficit Hyperactivity Disorder). At the University of California San Diego (UCSD) Shiley Eye Center, ophthalmologists and researchers have uncovered a relationship between a vision disorder called convergence insufficiency and AD/HD. Convergence insufficiency is a physical eye problem that makes it difficult to keep both eyes pointed and focused at a near target, thus making it hard to maintain concentration when reading.

According to David B. Granet, M.D., a UCSD School of Medicine associate professor of ophthalmology and pediatrics and director of the UCSD Ratner Children's Eye Center: "We showed that children with the disorder convergence insufficiency are three times as likely to be diagnosed with AD/HD than children without the disorder. This is the first time such a relationship has been identified between these two disorders."

When reviewing 266 charts of patients with convergence insufficiency, Dr. Granet and his colleagues found that 26 patients (9.8 percent) had been diagnosed with AD/HD some time in their lives. Of those, 20 patients (76.9 percent) were on medication for AD/HD when they were diagnosed with convergence insufficiency. "When we turned it around and looked at the AD/HD population, we found an almost 16 percent incidence of convergence insufficiency, or again more than three times what you'd expect [as compared to the fact that less than 5 percent of children are affected by convergence insufficiency]. The significance of this relationship is intriguing," says Dr. Granet. "We don't know if convergence insufficiency makes AD/HD worse or if convergence insufficiency is misdiagnosed as AD/HD. What we do know is that more research must be done on this subject and that patients diagnosed with AD/HD should also be evaluated for convergence insufficiency and treated accordingly. Further work may aid in understanding both disorders."[1]

Dr. Maria Lymberis, treasurer of the American Psychiatric Association, echoes those sentiments: "Hyperactivity is a very complex subject. All the ingredients have to be there if the brain is going to work properly. So you can think about what the people at the eye center are doing as one piece of the puzzle." Further, Dr. Lymberis says she would not be surprised if a relationship between the two disorders were eventually proved to exist. "It's not exactly a new idea. The brain is not one uniform thing. It is many centers with many different highly specialized functions. So if you're having a problem even in a relatively minor part of the circuitry, it can affect your overall attention performance."[2]

A study conducted by Dr. Michael W. Rouse and colleagues, published in the September 1999 issue of *Optometry and Vision Science*, found a relatively high prevalence of convergence insufficiency in the populations of fifth-grade and sixth-grade students they studied. Dr. Rouse, of the Southern California College of Optometry, noted that about 13 percent of the children given vision examinations in his study demonstrated either definite convergence insufficiency or were highly suspect for it.[3]

Psychiatrists and pediatricians need to become aware of the connection between vision and attention so that they can refer their patients to the appropriate experts dealing with AD/HD instead of just medicating children with stimulants such as Ritalin.

The process of vision is more than seeing with the eyes. While the eyes are an instrument of vision, vision itself is a fully body process. It is integrated with the development of the total child, influencing, among other things, posture, coordination, personality, and intelligence.

As I've helped AD/HD patients with their specifically vision-oriented problems (reading and writing, balance and coordination, for example) and learned more about AD/HD, I've seen how drug therapies simply are not helping. And so I've researched the conditions of my patients in depth and looked for an alternative, comprehensive, and nontoxic treatment.

Present-day medicine views AD/HD as having a variety of symptoms, but instead of the doctor reading the signs, symptoms, behaviors, and lab tests in an integrated fashion, the standard medical model is to treat the parts as a separate, segmented system. In addition, most of the profession, which has become more automated with advanced technology, is mechanistic at best, with the resultant loss of the humanistic aspect. One of the major factors influencing this trend is the advent of managed care, which requires doctors to see a high volume of patients in order to pay their costs and allow them to make a living. The days of the family doctor spending as much time as needed with each patient are dwindling. Most parents searching for answers for their child have expressed frustration about bouncing from one doctor to another. Although they are getting a good diagnostic work-up, little help is offered in terms of therapeutic value. Since the various doctors specialize in their own particular fields, they are unable to see the whole picture and put it together.

However, holistic medicine is a rapidly growing field. I would like to define the difference between holistic and alternative. There are a number of alternative practitioners who are not holistic. They may offer an alternative form of treatment, but their approaches have the same shortcomings as most of the medical doctors who practice mainstream medicine. They don't look at the whole person. It is critically important that parents who are seeking help for their children with symptoms of AD/HD find a health practitioner who encompasses the whole child in the treatment plan.

Because more parents are now seeking a medical model that does encompass holistic treatments for their children labeled with AD/HD, there has been a strong backlash against the use of drugs to treat attention and learning problems.

I have observed in such children an extraordinary capacity to overcome and, sometimes, fully resolve early developmental delays when they are given the tincture of time, family support, and proper environmental support. If we can take this approach, then AD/HD is no longer an appropriate label.

Over the years I've treated some five thousand patients with ADD and AD/HD. Their case histories show that, without exception, the nondrug therapies I've developed have helped them significantly. None of them now needs to rely on drug therapies. That's the strongest argument for my approach.

If you're struggling with ADD or AD/HD, I am certain that *Without Ritalin*, which describes our work in behavioral optometry, will help you.

# What Is ADD?

Attention Deficit Disorder (ADD) and Attention Deficit Hyperactivity Disorder (AD/HD) describe behavioral patterns that interfere with normal functioning and activities at home, in school, or at work. These valid disorders are neurological conditions that lead to various types of behavioral dysfunction.

## ADD Versus AD/HD

The American Psychiatric Association (APA) has compiled a list of symptoms associated with different forms of AD/HD, which include the inattentive type formerly called ADD and also AD/HD syndrome, the hyperactive/impulsive-type behavior. The APA has published these criteria in the fourth edition of the *Diagnostic and Statistical Manual of Mental Disorders* (DSM IV) to help doctors identify patients they suspect may have such attention problems. With so much confusion today about what to call attention problems, the most recognizable term is ADD, which explains all the different subtypes. But most health professionals refer to both ADD and AD/HD labels with the generic AD/HD term when discussing someone who is impulsive, inattentive, or hyperactive. I will be using the term AD/HD when discussing the disorders in this book.

AD/HD is the most common childhood behavioral disorder. It describes a person who shows concentration and attention problems resulting from some type of brain processing, developmental delay, or learning disorder. It also can describe a person who cannot sit quietly and shows behavioral dysfunctions. These behaviors can severely affect school performance, family relationships, and social interactions with peers. Based on the number of children receiving drug therapy for such behaviors, many school settings are now reporting a much higher incidence of AD/HD than in the past. And boys are more commonly identified with AD/HD than girls.

There are many possible causes for AD/HD. Genetics, neurotransmitter imbalances, heavy metal toxicities, and food sensitivities are all possible causative factors. But one of the problems with diagnosing AD/HD is that there is no definitive objective test, although the standard diagnostic tests for AD/HD include twelve behavioral patterns, as follows. The person:

1. Blurts out answers to questions before the questions have been completed
2. Loses patience when waiting their turn in group activities
3. Is very distractible by outside stimuli
4. Cannot remain seated when asked to do so
5. Fidgets with feet and hands
6. Cannot follow directions
7. Loses items often
8. Has attention difficulty
9. Talks too much
10. Cannot play quietly
11. Jumps quickly from one task to another
12. Does not listen[1]

Any child exhibiting eight of these twelve behaviors is diagnosed as AD/HD. But how do we define "very distractible," "fidgets," "often," "too much," "quickly," or "quietly"? These definitions, and therefore the diagnosis, are based on subjective criteria that depend to a large extent on the bias, personality, and experience of the diagnosing doctor.

Though most doctors view AD/HD as a malfunction of the brain and the neurological system of the body, they hardly ever do neurological testing before prescribing Ritalin. Instead, they all too often simply base their diagnoses on the observations and experiences of teachers and parents. The diagnosis of AD/HD is based entirely on behavioral, subjective, and nonmedical data instead of medical examination and testing, which give a more accurate picture of the whole person.

A number of studies show that when a parent, teacher, or clinician rate the same child their scores vary significantly. The APA criteria for AD/HD officially points a finger at children who "interrupt others" and "cannot follow instructions." One of the scales widely used by parents to diagnose AD/HD is the Revised Conner's Questionnaire, which says children are suspected to be hyperactive if they are "sassy" or "wanting to run things." Conner's goes so far as to say that if children act "childish" they have AD/HD.[2] These criteria encourage parents to dismiss the innate personality of particular children who may have a strong sense of their own inner rhythm and timing. Perhaps they feel frustrated by authoritarian attitudes toward them. Are they merely reacting to rules set up in an autocratic system?

These broad and flexible (i.e., subjective) definitions given by some to AD/HD have certain advantages for doctors, parents, and schools. Once the diagnosis of AD/HD is made, a doctor may prescribe drug treatment, and one more patient is "satisfactorily" accounted for. From the parents' point of view, an AD/HD diagnosis comfortably explains the errant behavior of a seemingly troubled, misbehaving child. Teachers, also, too often support the AD/HD diagnosis and subsequent drug therapy because they control potentially disruptive elements in the classroom.

In one recent study reported in the *American Journal of Public Health*, the criteria for diagnosing AD/HD varied significantly across the U.S. population. The study, which included a group of students in grades two through five in school districts that used medication to treat AD/HD, concluded that there was an overdiagnosis and an overtreatment of AD/HD in some groups of these children.[3]

Sadly, however, my personal and quite extensive experience shows that both ADD and AD/HD are labels that limit a child's development and potential. Instead of standardized labeling, I believe that we need to examine the behavioral patterns defined as AD/HD, discover the reasons for them, find the causative imbalances in a person's mind/body, and treat them individually. After all, each child is first and foremost a unique individual. It is our obligation to treat them as such in every way, not the least of which are medical and diagnostic.

## Increased Diagnoses and Prescriptions

While more and more children seem to be displaying learning, reading, writing, and behavioral problems, the idea of classification is not new. AD/HD is just the latest in a long line of labels that has been used to classify "difficult" children. Other classifications include learning disability, scotopic sensitivity syndrome, developmental delay, autism, sensory motor integration dysfunction, dyslexia, disorders in writing and speaking, slow learner, hypoactivity, hyperactivity, and convergence insufficiency.

But the increasingly common diagnosis of AD/HD prompts several questions. Are the conditions usually associated with AD/HD actually occurring more frequently, or are they being conveniently diagnosed as AD/HD more frequently?

I suspect that children today are being diagnosed and drugged psychiatrically because they don't fit into society's structure or follow the rules that say how they should act. This form of treatment not only suppresses a child's creativity and uniqueness, it also robs humankind of their special gifts.

If our children are indeed too boisterous, perhaps our society is responsible for some of their overstimulation. Children spend more hours playing Nintendo and watching TV than ever before. Movies are more violent. There is a growing atmosphere of urgency, intensity, and haste. We eat fast food, drive fast cars, and use caffeine and other amphetamine-type substances to amp ourselves up for everyday life.

Although there may be disagreement about the reasons for the increasing numbers of AD/HD diagnoses, these are the facts:

- The number of children taking Ritalin is doubling every two years.[4]
- Two million children diagnosed with AD/HD take Ritalin today.[5]
- Consumers spent $373 million on Ritalin and its generic counterparts in 1996.[6]
- Production of Ritalin by drug companies has increased by nearly 500 percent in the last five years.[7]

Any way you look at it, AD/HD presents some serious problems to us all. While I am deeply concerned about the widespread use of drug therapy for AD/HD, I do not underestimate the effects of the behaviors associated with AD/HD and the misery they can create for individuals and within families. Whether we're parents, teachers, therapists, or doctors, our biggest concern must be how to handle the conditions associated with AD/HD without physically or psychologically damaging those who exhibit the symptoms.

## The Value of an Observant Teacher or Parent

What is the best screening device to detect AD/HD? An observant parent will see certain behaviors and characteristics that point to a problem. Most mothers know that something is different about their children's behavior at a very young age, even before they enter school. I have found that most behavioral problems begin to occur between the ages of three and four, often before a child starts preschool.

Teachers play important roles in identifying whether a child might have a developmental-learning problem, as they routinely evaluate a child's work habits, their off-task behaviors, organizational skills, social skills, and the manner in which they handle their responsibilities. Often a teacher is the first person to suspect a child may have a learning or behavioral problem and may seek assistance from the school nurse or school psychologist to help evaluate the child.

If you suspect your child may have AD/HD, it is important to involve a team of professionals who can test your child's IQ; developmental motor skills, which include sensory processing and cognitive processing; and body biochemistry. Using a multidisciplinary team of professionals will help to develop a comprehensive picture of your child, which can be used to get help that includes more than just treating symptoms.

One of the key tip-offs that parents may look for in their children is that they behave differently from other children their own age. In their book *Driven to Distraction*, Edward Hallowell, M.D., and John Ratey, M.D., explain that a person's AD/HD behavior may be diagnosed based on a comparison with a group of his peers. They report that AD/HD children are much more inattentive and restless and exhibit more high-energy behavior than their peers and that this behavior usually surfaces before age seven and has persisted for at least six months. Drs. Hallowell and Ratey also state that AD/HD behaviors must be intense enough to be disabling to the child.

Although an accurate diagnosis and medication have brought help to thousands, most health professionals who specialize in AD/HD agree that stimulant medication is not the answer. Drugs clearly only treat the symptoms, and if a child's medication is discontinued the behaviors reappear. Further, the toxicity of the drug can affect the brain, the liver, and the entire biochemistry of the body. Parents, teachers, and doctors are better off in the long run to look for the causative factors that might be influencing the behavior of the child.

An excellent support organization, called P.A.V.E. (Parents Active for Vision Education), has published a behavioral checklist that can help pinpoint certain visually related learning problems in school-age children. If you suspect that you or your child may suffer from AD/HD, please complete the following comprehensive checklist.

## Behavioral Characteristics

### Physical Clues
- ☐ Red, sore, itching eyes
- ☐ Erratic eye movements
- ☐ Squinting or excessive eye rubbing
- ☐ Blurred or double vision
- ☐ Head tilting, closing, or blocking one eye when reading

### Performance Clues
- ☐ Avoidance of reading and near work
- ☐ Frequent loss of place
- ☐ Rereads letters or words
- ☐ Difficulty recognizing the same word in the next sentence
- ☐ Letter or word reversals
- ☐ Difficulty copying from the board
- ☐ Poor handwriting
- ☐ Book held too close to the eyes
- ☐ Poor or inconsistent sports performance

### Inattentiveness
- ☐ Difficulty organizing tasks—can't get started
- ☐ Mental restlessness—constant mental chatter
- ☐ Easily distracted—attention easily diverted
- ☐ Difficulty completing tasks
- ☐ Shifts from one task to another
- ☐ Difficulty sustaining attention—unable to focus
- ☐ Doesn't listen to others

☐ Loses possessions constantly
☐ Forgets constantly—can't remember what to do
☐ Trouble keeping track of events
☐ Poor sequencing
☐ Hyperactive
☐ Talks too much
☐ Difficulty doing tasks alone
☐ Physical restlessness—finger-tapping, leg restlessness
☐ Always on the go—driven like a motor
☐ Likes daring activities
☐ Often interrupts others
☐ Unpredictable behavior
☐ Hot and explosive temper
☐ Impulsive

# Drug Therapy

## ∞ John's Story

John had been a problem child since age two. His medical history included several ear infections, severe eczema that had required hospitalization twice, and asthma. When John started school, he had a difficult time fitting in. His teachers described him as disruptive and boisterous. He could not sit still in the classroom and had a hard time following directions. Physically, he was very clumsy and awkward. When the school gave him educational tests, he scored two years below his age level. John's handwriting was poor, and he was falling further behind in school.

A guidance counselor recommended John's mother take him to see a neurologist to confirm the diagnosis of AD/HD. The neurologist ran a few tests and prescribed Ritalin, the standard drug therapy for AD/HD. Taking the drug for a few weeks, John's behavior became more agitated. So his mother took him to see a second doctor. This doctor discontinued the Ritalin and prescribed Dexedrine for John. With this new drug, John was not sleeping or eating, and he seemed unmotivated. Seeking the help of a third doctor, John's mother took him to see a specialist in psychiatry. This doctor decided John was depressed and prescribed Prozac. But John's mother became concerned after reading various health-related magazine articles about the side effects of Prozac. When she questioned the doctor about what she'd read, he dismissed the articles as "anecdotal" and advised her "not to read too much."

Knowing that her son was not improving, John's mother took him to three more specialists and spent thousands of dollars during the next year. John received a battery of psychological and educational tests, but still there were no convincing answers.

John's story is typical, and it illustrates many of the problems associated with drug therapy.

## Drug Therapies for AD/HD

The standard drug therapy for AD/HD revolves around four major stimulant drugs: Ritalin, Dexedrine, Desoxyn, and Cylert. Stimulant medications have shown to have a 60 to 80 percent short-term effectiveness in controlling hyperactivity, distractibility, and impulsivity in school-age children.[1] Adults diagnosed with AD/HD have found that stimulant medications improve body coordination, handwriting, and attention span.

When these stimulants fail to control behavior, antidepressants are used. There is also an increased use of clonidine, a blood pressure medication gaining popularity as a treatment for insomnia associated with attention disorders.

Medications have been used for sixty years to treat behavioral and learning problems. Presently there are five classes of drugs being used for children with learning and behavioral problems.

The first class of drugs, called psychostimulants, include Ritalin, Cylert, Dexedrine, and ADDerol. These stimulant drugs seem to have the opposite effect on people with symptoms of AD/HD by calming and relaxing their behavior. However, an article in *Exceptional Children,* which reviewed the use of stimulant medications for the treatment of ADD, showed that these drugs affect dopamine levels and thus activate the part of the brain that helps to regulate the arousal system.

The second class of drugs include antidepressants such as Prozac, imipramine, Wellbutrin, and Anafranil. These drugs influence serotonin levels in the brain and other neurotransmitters and thus help to reduce anxiety and socially unacceptable behaviors.

The next set of drugs are antihypertensives, such as clonidine and Tenex, which can reduce blood pressure, help calm the body, and improve the sleep cycle. Anticonvulsives are also used to relax patients, even if there is no spiking on their EEGs, or in the absence of seizures.

The last set of drugs are antipsychotics, which help to lessen behaviors such as aggression, hallucinations, and agitation. Many times these classes of drugs are used in various combinations to balance out each other's side effects. For example, Ritalin can cause sleep problems, so clonidine is added to assist sleep. Combining these drugs can cause disastrous results.

## Increased Usage of Stimulants and Antidepressants

"Kids and Pills," a special report in *USA Weekend,* showed that Ritalin and Prozac are being prescribed increasingly for children. *The New York Times* reported that the "three Rs" of school are now reading, writing, and Ritalin. And toddlers are now being given Prozac, Ritalin, and other powerful drugs to control behavioral problems.

Many medical experts call it "troubling" and "very surprising" that the number of preschoolers taking stimulants, antidepressants, and other psychiatric drugs increased drastically from 1991 to 1995. There was a twofold to threefold increase in the use of Ritalin among children ages two through four who were enrolled in two state Medicaid programs and in an HMO in the Northwest.[2] The number of preschoolers receiving prescriptions for antidepressants doubled in the Medicaid programs. A study published in the *American Journal of Public Health* was the first to document increased prescription drug use among children younger than five years of age, based on research analyzing the prescription records of more than 200,000 preschoolers in two Medicaid programs and an HMO during a five-year period.[3]

Drugs prescribed by doctors for purposes not approved by the FDA, called off-label prescribing, is both legal and common in the treatment of older children, but this practice raises more particular concerns for younger children. Research on the safety and efficacy of such medications—which already is limited even for older children—has not been conducted at all for preschoolers. And most parents don't even realize off-label prescribing is done.

Though well-meaning medical experts are very sympathetic in attempting to do something for children having difficulty controlling their behavior or who are terribly sick, managed care will not pay for counseling or other treatments that don't involve drugs. The enormous pressure for teachers, parents, and schools to diagnose children with AD/HD has resulted in drugs being the preferred mode of treatment because prescription drugs are the only form of treatment covered by managed care. Payment will be made only for visits to a primary care physician instead of visits to a specialist for treatment.

Furthermore, diagnosing the symptoms of emotional or behavioral problems displayed by children younger than five is far from exact. Dr. Joseph Coyle, chairman of psychiatry at Harvard Medical School, explains that the normal behavior of many two- and three-year-old children looks a lot like AD/HD even though these children don't have this problem.

I question how these children can qualify for the diagnostic criteria for AD/HD or depression at such a young age. And what is the justification for giving them stimulants, antidepressants, and clonidine? Even more serious is the fact that researchers don't know how these drugs affect brain development during a critical time period for brain and sensory-motor development, as well as learning development, in preschoolers.

One study showed that Ritalin accounted for 90 percent of the prescriptions written for preschoolers.[4] In a Midwestern Medicaid group, 11.1 of every 1,000 children within the two- to five-year-old age group were prescribed Ritalin in 1995.[5] In an HMO and a mid-Atlantic Medicaid group, the number of girls receiving prescriptions for stimulants increased more in five years than the number of boys, suggesting that girls are increasingly being diagnosed with attention disorders.[6] AD/HD is no longer only a little boys' disease.

One has to wonder if these preschoolers being medicated because of "severe behavioral problems" are also suffering from asthma, diabetes, and other major chronic illnesses. Or are they suffering from developmental delays and sensory-motor integration processing problems or autism? Many doctors prescribe drugs as a last-ditch effort to control behavior, but we need to look a little deeper into why children are on a downward spiral.

Change is on the horizon. The National Institute of Mental Health announced that it would spend six million dollars over the next five years to study whether Ritalin is safe and effective for children under the age of six.[7]

## Drugs Are Not the Answer

While the increased use of drug therapy seems to indicate that it is effective, let's consider the downside. Every day about 3 to 5 percent of children who attend school are taking cocaine-derived Ritalin to alter their minds and their behavior, because the drug makes them more goal-oriented or task-directed.[8] But so what? Ritalin does nothing to improve academic achievement or to improve learning or reading.

I have observed children on Ritalin. Although it allows them to sit more calmly, or perhaps imitate the behavior of sitting quietly, they look as though they are disconnected and isolated. Remember, when

Ritalin is used to control behavior it suppresses symptoms and conceals the imbalances causing the behavioral "problems," as well.

Peter Breggin, M.D., a psychiatrist and author of *The War Against Children*, argues strongly that Ritalin is dangerously overprescribed. He believes that these stimulant drugs are harmful and can cause side effects in the body. *The Physicians' Desk Reference* (PDR) lists twenty-five side effects of Ritalin, including anxiety, hair loss, nausea, headaches, weight loss, and interruption of growth. Some patients on Ritalin become compulsive, for example, biting their nails until bleeding occurs. Other side effects include high blood pressure, increased heart rate, and Tourette's syndrome—which exhibits in repetitive involuntary movements called tics, usually of the head, neck, face, eyes, and mouth.

Potentially even more dangerous are the possible effects of Ritalin on the brain's growth. Because this subject has not been adequately researched, we have no knowledge of how Ritalin may inhibit brain growth, much of which occurs during the years when Ritalin is usually prescribed for children suspected of having AD/HD.

Ciba Geigy, the manufacturer of Ritalin, says it is not habit forming, but the Drug Enforcement Agency classifies it as a Schedule II drug with potential for misuse. Although the PDR states that Ritalin should not be prescribed for children under age six, in 1993 U.S. physicians wrote 200,000 prescriptions for Ritalin and other stimulant drugs for children five years old and younger.[9] Ritalin has been prescribed for children as young as eighteen months old.

Drugs such as Ritalin can affect some short-term behavioral control, but it is a superficial healing at best. Ritalin does not treat the root cause. It may reduce stress for the caregiver, for the child, for teachers, and even for doctors, but it condemns the patient to the likelihood of being tied to this toxic therapy for life. That might be acceptable if there were no other choices. But there are other choices, proven and effective. And in light of this, it seems both medically and ethically unacceptable to continue to rely so heavily on drug therapies.

## Long-Term Effects

Despite its widespread use, neither The National Institute of Health nor Ritalin's manufacturer know exactly what Ritalin's long-term side effects might be. Dr. Peter Breggin reports in *The War Against Children* that one study found brain shrinkage in AD/HD-labeled adults who had been taking Ritalin for years, with the authors of the study suggesting "cortical atrophy may be a long-term adverse effect of Ritalin treatment."[10]

Do we really want to give our children a drug which may atrophy their brains? And surely there is a terrible irony in the fact that such a possibly brain-damaging drug should be given to people who are thought to have some kind of "brain problem" in the first place.

## Why Is Ritalin So Heavily Prescribed?

Drugs are big business. The fact that about 85 percent of children diagnosed with AD/HD today receive drug therapy is evidence that some drug companies have turned AD/HD into a billion-dollar industry. Drug companies have a symbiotic relationship with doctors. At medical conferences, free samples of their products are handed out like Halloween candy. This is an effective marketing tool to keep the drugs' names in front of doctors so that when they are faced with an AD/HD diagnosis they automatically reach for their prescription pads. The overwhelming financial interests and power of the drug companies stifle knowledge of other forms of treatment. The model of drug therapy is fast and easy. It's profitable for everyone involved—except the patient. It's ingrained in the doctor's education. Until doctors are willing to seek alternatives, they will continue to practice the standard way of drug therapy.

The medical profession and drug companies are not the only participants with a vested interest in Ritalin and its allied drugs. As the pace of life becomes faster we seem to expect schools and day-care centers to baby-sit our children. If a child has a behavioral problem, many of these institutions recommend the quickest, easiest fix, even if it is ultimately damaging to those in their care. Numerous reports indicate that both private and public schools strongly recommend drug treatment for a "difficult" child. Schools routinely refer parents to specific doctors who favor prescribing drugs. Some schools threaten to take drastic measures if the parents of a "difficult" child do not put them on Ritalin—even refusing to allow the child into the classroom.

While all of these pressures result in drugs being prescribed to children for treatment of AD/HD at a rate doubling every two years, Ciba Geigy explains away the increase in the drug's use as being due to "heightened public awareness." However, the most popular AD/HD support group is C.H.A.D.D. (Children and Adults with Attention Deficit Disorder), an organization that sponsors lectures recommending conventional medical treatment rather than alternative or holistic methods. Because Ciba Geigy has made significant monetary contributions to C.H.A.D.D., it seems fair to question whether the "heightened public awareness" has been created largely by Ciba Geigy itself and to be suspicious of the fact that this support group often recommends medications to parents, Ritalin first and foremost.

I am not an alarmist or a conspiracy theorist, but there is no doubt in my mind that, effectively, there is collusion between the drug companies, doctors, and schools. It may not be planned. It may be coincidental. But it has resulted in the almost irresistible promotion of drug therapy and the comprehensive stifling of any alternative, non-drug treatment for AD/HD.

Fortunately, there is hope. There are alternatives to drug treatment. *Without Ritalin* offers methods of treatment for AD/HD without the side effects of either stimulant or antidepressant drug therapies.

# There Is Hope!

## ∞ John's Story—A Happy Ending

John's mother felt increasingly more desperate as each new prescription and each new drug seemed only to make her son's condition worse. Determined to find help for John, she carefully read a magazine article suggesting natural and holistic methods for treating AD/HD, which a friend had given her. The article explained how drug therapy only treats symptoms, not the underlying causes, and that patients need to take responsibility for their own wellness, not just rely on doctors for all the answers. The article also explained that toxins in the body interfere with the body's opportunity to return to balance; that drug therapy only contributes to this so-called virtual toxic waste dump in the body; and that the resulting biochemical imbalances can lead to significant behavioral and learning problems.

Eventually John's mother found her way to me. During the initial evaluation I explained that I treat AD/HD by using a more holistic approach and insisted that John's mother share an equal partnership in the management of John's health.

First, an extensive history was taken, including John's medical, prenatal, developmental, and academic details. A list of John's daily food intake was also needed. Because of his academic problems, John's sensory-motor development was tested. The results indicated that, although he was nine years old chronologically, developmentally he processed information at the level of a five-year-old. This was an obvious indicator that John was being expected to work at a basic skill level that was far too advanced for his abilities. In order to help John develop better gross motor skills, which could enable better learning in school, I prescribed a developmental learning program of exercises, which John and his mother did every day for one hour.

A biochemical analysis I ordered showed that John's body contained extremely high levels of the heavy metals copper, aluminum, and iron. He also suffered from hypoglycemia and adrenal exhaustion. John was put on a detoxification program and given a regimen of vitamins and minerals. We also found some food allergies and treated them.

Today John is a high school senior and has been accepted to attend Stanford University, where he plans to study engineering.

## ∞ Melissa's Story

Melissa suffered a head trauma as she was coming down the birth canal. As a young child she had insomnia, ear infections, temper tantrums, and asthma. At eleven years of age she was twenty pounds overweight, very lethargic, and a slow reader. She had been diagnosed with AD/HD, and if her parents had followed what has become standard procedure, Melissa would have been the perfect candidate for treatment with Ritalin. Instead, Melissa's parents brought her to me.

After running various behavioral and physical tests, we discovered that the underlying causes of Melissa's conditions were developmental motor coordination problems, heavy metal toxicity, hypoglycemia, and food allergies. (The effects of biochemistry on the body will be discussed in detail in chapter 6.) Melissa was given herbs and homeopathic remedies to help her body detoxify. She was counseled to change her diet and participate in a developmental learning program (discussed in chapters 7 and 9).

Within five months Melissa lost over fifteen pounds, gained energy and self-esteem, made honor roll at school, and became a star in volleyball and soccer.

In Melissa's case AD/HD was a fundamental misdiagnosis, the direct result of conveniently grouping an array of symptoms under the all-embracing AD/HD label.

## ∞ David's Story

David had a traumatic birth. His umbilical cord was wrapped around his neck, forceps were needed to assist in his delivery, and he suffered anoxia (lack of oxygen) and severe jaundice at birth. As a young child David never crawled, and he was clumsy during physical activities. He had suffered many sinus infections, sore throats, and colds as a child. His mother reported he was constantly on antibiotics.

At age nine David was diagnosed with AD/HD, and the school psychologist diagnosed him as having a learning disability in written and verbal expression. During his schoolwork David would jump ahead when reading and speaking, he showed careless work habits, and he had very poor handwriting skills. David was prescribed Dexedrine for his impulsivity, but his parents were concerned about the long-term side effects of the medication. He was referred by one of his reading tutors to our office for an evaluation.

In order to develop a profile of David, his mother and father filled out a detailed questionnaire on his digestive, nervous, immune, cardiovascular, and sensory-motor systems. After each category was scored, a treatment plan was created based on David's history, symptoms, and evaluation of the answers on the questionnaire. David's diet consisted of macaroni and cheese, Coca-Cola, ice cream, and pancakes. Therefore, we decided to address his nutrition first. David, his parents, and I agreed on the following treatment plan.

David was referred to a nutritionist who could help him develop a diet that would better support his digestion and absorption and at the same time improve his detoxification pathway so he could release any environmental and other pollutants from his body. In addition, homeopathic remedies would be used instead of Dexedrine.

David was referred to an osteopathic physician for cranial sacral therapy. Based on his birth history, I thought structural therapy would help release his birth trauma and relieve some of the stress in his head and neck areas.

Improving David's sensory-motor skills was also important. First, he worked in a program called Fast ForWord—an auditory processing program that enhances the auditory timing mechanism of the brain to allow for more rapid language building. I knew Fast ForWord would help David learn to discriminate and recognize different phonemes at a variety of speeds and achieve more flexibility in this area. I also worked with David in a visual-learning development program to help him integrate his visual-motor skills.

A few months ago I received a letter from David, who is now a senior at Michigan State University, studying chemical engineering. He wrote that he is feeling great and very excited about his career possibilities. Most important, he feels like a normal person and enjoys his college experience very much. He has let go of his AD/HD diagnosis.

As you can see in these three case histories, we approach a person diagnosed with AD/HD from a holistic perspective. Part of this perspective involves looking at the total development as it relates to learning and intelligence. The next step is to understand how development affects a child's learning ability.

# AD/HD and the Development of Intelligence

Before we discuss the holistic treatment of AD/HD, it's valuable to examine the behavioral and intellectual development of a child because an apparent difficulty in such development causes so many children to be labeled dysfunctional with AD/HD.

We begin to study behavior with the development of vision. Educational psychologists have found that 70 to 90 percent of all learning in school comes through the eyes.[1] We call this vision. Arnold Gesell, M.D., a child development expert, said: "So interfused are vision and the action system that the two must be regarded as inseparable. To understand vision, we must know the child; to understand the child, we must know the nature of his vision."[2]

## What Is Vision?

Vision is more than eyes. It is part of the interrelated sensory-motor system in the brain. This includes the vestibular (relating to balance), motor (movement), speech/language, auditory (hearing), and tactile (touch) functions. The sensory-motor system reflects the neurological development of the child. This system begins in utero and goes through certain developmental phases in order for normal function to occur. Sensory-motor skills are learned and developed. If a child has not developed these skills by school age, then adaptations occur. Adaptations are a natural process that help children learn and grow. Children reach a point where they can no longer move forward, and this forces them to make an adjustment in how they see or do something in order to find a new way of seeing it or doing it.

One of the key factors in child development is the nervous system. The nervous system comprises an interconnected network of nerve cells that communicate and work together throughout the body. The brain, of course, is an area with an extraordinarily high concentration of nerve cells.

An essential part of child development is the child's relationship with his environment. Children take in sensations from the environment, process these through the brain, and organize and integrate these sensations using their bodies. This process can be observed as behavior. A child's brain, as the traffic director, takes sensory information from the world and organizes this information to form perceptions, behaviors, and learning.

Dr. Gesell described vision as a developing system that has a basic genetic pattern but is also highly influenced by environment. Vision, according to Gesell, is a full body process. It is integrated with the development of the total child, influencing posture, coordination, personality, and intelligence.

The analysis of a child by doctors of behavioral optometry goes far beyond optical correction and checking eye health. Acuity is only one aspect in the development of vision. It is also vital to consider how the development of the child's vision relates to the other neurological and sensory systems. The complex task of reading requires that the eyes, neck muscles, and inner ear all work. Integration of these senses begins prenatally, in the womb, when the fetus feels gravity through the mother's body.

## The Fetus and Sensory-Motor Development

The development of a child's vision begins as a fetus in utero. At eighteen days old the human embryo is about one-eighth-inch long, but the eyes are recognizable as bulges on the developing brain. At one month, the optic vesicles (comprised of these bulges) have fully invaginated. Also, at this time, the cerebral hemispheres are fully present. Up to about the fourth month of development of the fetus, there is a close relationship between the cortex of the brain and the cells of the retina. The eyes and vision originate from brain cells; when we work with vision, we are working with an extension of the brain.

The eyes are created as a dialogue between the developing brain and the skin of the embryo. The front of the brain sends out a hollow stem on each side. The stem forms a vesicle. When the vesicle approaches the surface of the skin it turns inward like a cup. This cup becomes the retina of the eye.

In the fetus's fourth week a bubble turns inward from the skin on both sides of the rear of the brain. This bubble becomes the inner ear, with its auditory and balance organs.

Certain reflexes, such as grasping, clinging, and sucking, are important and necessary skills. As soon as the nerves and muscles have been established in the earliest fetal stage, grasping and sucking are frequent, kicking and waving begin as strength is increased, and impulse patterns are perfected. The surging, dark amniotic fluid environment of the uterus stimulates the development of the fetus's peripheral vision, as vision becomes the steering mechanism that helps the body move through space. It aids us with orientation (knowing where we are in our world), localization (seeing details), and understanding gravity and balance.

Since all the sensory systems are highly integrated throughout the brain and body, if there is a developmental delay in one system it will ultimately affect the rest. In order for the child to become a proficient learner, he needs to be able to control his body. We call this mind/body control. Until this happens, a child will not be able to learn the more abstract concepts such as reading and writing.

Sally Goddard, a neuropsychologist at the Institute for Neuro-Physiological Psychology in England, has found that children who exhibit constant internal excitation also have increased muscle tension. She says that prolonged muscle tension causes eventual fatigue, which will reduce performance. A child then will have to increase her level of arousal to continue to perform. Therefore, a vicious cycle is created. To overcome tiredness, the child must increase movement—using movement and momentum as a way to recharge her batteries. It's a survival mechanism. The sympathetic nervous system is over-worked, while the parasympathetic nervous system (the resting part of the nervous system) is not allowed to work. The nervous system becomes out of balance. Goddard believes stimulants such as Ritalin calm a child's hyperactivity by artificially stimulating their self-induced arousal system.

She has found that the development of sensory-motor skills is also highly influenced by prenatal development. If the brain poorly organizes and integrates these systems, then the child never develops the foundational sensory-motor processing skills. Without that ground-work, the more complex tasks of reading, writing, and academic achievement can be severely limited. The primitive survival reflexes in utero have a strong effect on a child's learning potential. Goddard says that if the primitive reflexes are not inhibited, then a child will be more reflexive and less voluntary with controlling her senses. She defines attention-deficit children as those who have to pay attention to every stimulus in the room.

## Primitive Survival Reflexes

The primitive survival reflexes, which originate in the brain stem (not higher up in the brain cortex), are automatic movements that help newborns adjust to the overwhelming amount of stimuli they encounter once they leave their mothers' wombs. The primitive reflexes may be viewed as learning experiences for the newborn, which act as a foundation for more complex muscle movements. However, these primitive reflexes should have a limited life span of six to twelve months. If these reflexes linger beyond this period, they impede normal sensory development and interfere with the general and specific motor skills of a child.

Athletes who still have their primitive reflexes become proficient with a certain specific motor movement as a splinter skill, but they don't have the flexibility to integrate other movements. Lack of inhibition of these reflexes will cause vision problems. Usually, the eye movements are very poor, and there is difficulty shifting from near to far.

Primitive survival reflex therapy was brought from Sweden to this country by two Scandinavian eye doctors who received their training from Catherina Johanneson-Alvegard, the therapy's developer. Drs. Lena Reuterhall and Thorkild Rasmussen have found that not only are primitive survival reflexes important for the in utero development of the fetus but also affect the neurodevelopment necessary for proper vision and learning.

These primitive reflexes help infants identify what they see in front of them, coordinate both eyes (make them work together), and aid in focusing and depth perception. Visual problems at a later age often can be attributed to lingering primitive reflexes.

The reflexes, which have a limited, sequential, and very important life span, should be phased out within one year after delivery. And they should be phased out in a certain order. If they don't develop at the proper time or aren't phased out at the proper time, they will interfere with the higher cortical control of the brain. Lack of inhibition of the primitive reflexes will affect creeping, crawling, rolling, and general and ocular motor control.

The birth experience is another factor that affects the life span of the primitive reflexes: premature, breech, or C-section births can affect the sequential order of learning.

## Five Primitive Reflexes

Let us look at five of the primitive reflexes that most affect sensory motor development: the Moro reflex, the tonic labyrinthine reflex, the spinal galant reflex, the asymmetrical tonic neck reflex, and the symmetrical tonic neck reflex:

### The Moro Reflex

- Occurs at nine weeks in utero
- Should be inhibited at two to four months
- Is an involuntary reflex to threat

This survival mechanism is composed of a series of rapid movements of the arms upward away from the body. It is the earliest to emerge and forms a strong foundation for future life experience. However, a retained Moro reflex can cause vestibular-related problems such as poor balance and coordination. It can also cause visual-motor processing problems and biochemical and nutritional imbalances. As to the latter, there is a higher incidence of ear and throat infections, which lead to lower immunity and allergies. This pattern depletes energy and can cause fatigue and mood swings.

### CASE HISTORY: The Moro Reflex

Terry is a five-year-old who experiences the world as being too bright and too loud. She has difficulty in social situations and usually withdraws. She gets motion sickness very easily and cannot ride her bike because of poor balance. She has problems with visual fixation and shows excessive blinking. She avoids eye contact. Terry also suffers from asthma, eczema, and frequent ear infections. She has tense muscles and is very inflexible. She likes to feel in control and manipulates events to do so.

### The Tonic Labyrinthine Reflex (TLR)

- Occurs at sixteen weeks in utero
- Gradually inhibited, beginning at six weeks until three years of age

During this time there is a simultaneous development of the postural reflexes and more advanced movements. When an infant is able to raise and lower his head with his neck muscles, he begins to work with gravity. As this movement occurs automatically, the inhibition of the tonic labyrinthine reflex (TLR) begins. If the TLR lingers, it can cause poor balance, weak muscle tone, and visual-motor processing problems.

### CASE HISTORY: The Tonic Labyrinthine Reflex

Eddie is a six-year-old with many developmental delays. His posture is poor (he stoops over). He has weak muscle tone and usually gets carsick. He hates physical education class and avoids all sports. He forgets his homework and has a disorganized, messy room. Eddie has a tendency to walk on his toes. He is a poor reader. When writing he holds his head up by leaning it on one hand. This is a classic TLR profile.

### The Spinal Galant Reflex

- Occurs at twenty weeks in utero
- Inhibited at nine months

The spinal galant reflex (in conjunction with the asymmetrical tonic neck reflex) is used in the birthing process by helping the baby work its way through the birth canal. This reflex also enables the fetus to hear and feel the sound vibrations in the aquatic environment of the womb. If the spinal galant reflex lingers beyond the neonate period, it interferes with the ability of the child to control his bladder, which can cause bed-wetting beyond the age of five. In adults, some studies suggest that if the spinal galant reflex is still present it causes irritable bowel syndrome. Usually the behaviors seen in school-age children include fidgeting in their seats, squirming, or wiggling. Children also don't like clothing to fit tightly around the waist. This reflex is always competing with the child's attention and short-term memory because the child is distracted by the need to be in constant motion.

### CASE HISTORY: The Spinal Galant Reflex

Josh is an eight-year-old who is always fidgeting in class. His teacher describes his behavior as having "ants in his pants." He suffers from terrible concentration and problems with memory, especially short-term memory. He is a bed wetter, and his walking shows that he has a hip rotation to one side. Josh was diagnosed with an abnormal curvature of the spine.

### The Asymmetrical Tonic Neck Reflex (ATNR)

- Occurs at eighteen weeks in utero
- Inhibited at six months

In utero, the ATNR helps the fetus move its head from side to side while swinging its arms and kicking its legs. This pattern helps develop the muscle tone and the vestibular system. The reflex is needed at birth so that the fetus can help "unscrew" itself through the birth canal. This twisting movement is the first experience the infant has to understand coordinating both sides of the body together in a twisting action. Children taken by C-section are at a higher risk for developmental delay because without experiencing this twisting action through the birth canal they do not get the necessary bilateral integration that is needed for developing the later skills of crawling, walking, and skipping with the cross-patterning movement. There is more of a problem with balance and confusion with midline and mixed laterality.

### CASE HISTORY: The Asymmetrical Tonic Neck Reflex

Jason is a nine-year-old who still confuses his right and his left sides. When running or skipping he uses a homolateral (same side) movement with his arms and legs. Consequently, he has a difficult time skiing, ice skating, and roller blading. He is confused with his midline and tries to do everything with his right side. He plays soccer but can't seem to kick with his left foot very well. Sometimes he loses his balance easily and bumps into objects when he walks or runs. Jason skips words and letters when he tries to read and ends up rereading his assignments. His handwriting is illegible, and he cannot express his ideas on paper very easily. He has been diagnosed with convergence insufficiency. This could be a classic case of a child labeled with AD/HD.

### The Symmetrical Tonic Neck Reflex (STNR)

- Occurs at six to nine months after birth
- Inhibited at nine to eleven months
- Helps the infant learn to rise up on hands and knees
- If it lingers too long it will interfere with the infant's ability to learn creeping and crawling

STNR relates to creeping, which has been proven to be one of the most important movement patterns to help train the eyes to cross the midline of the body. As an infant begins to move from one hand to another, this movement trains the eyes to focus from one side to the other. Later, when a child is learning to read, she needs to have the skill of moving her eyes across the middle of the page without losing her place. Studies have shown that children who don't learn to creep and crawl have a higher incidence of reading and learning problems. Creeping and crawling are essential for visual development.

### CASE HISTORY: The Symmetrical Tonic Neck Reflex

Marge is a seven-year-old who has been described as a very clumsy child. She has a great deal of difficulty copying from the board and cannot shift her focus from near to far and back to near very easily. She shows poor swimming skills even though she has had swimming lessons. Her mother describes her as a messy eater, and she is always correcting Marge to sit up straight.

## Eye Movements, the Vestibular System, and Balance

In 1962, Dr. Hollie McHugh worked with five hundred children who had been referred to the Hearing and Language Disorders study group of Montreal Children's hospital. She found in her study that the majority of these children had hearing, vision, and vestibular (balance-related) problems. Using a sensory-motor approach to these problems, her results were astounding.[3]

Let's look at balance more closely. Balance is the core of functioning. It is the first system to be fully developed, becoming operational at sixteen weeks in utero and providing the fetus with a sense of direction and orientation in the womb. It helps the child deal with the force of gravity. If a mother is inactive during pregnancy, the fetus does not experience movement and orientation while in the womb, which are vital for experiencing the effects of gravity.

Gravity provides us with our center, whether it is in space, time, motion, or depth. As the infant develops, problems in balance will have repercussions for all other areas of functioning. Such problems affect the sensory systems because all sensation passes through the vestibular mechanism at the brain stem level before being transmitted elsewhere for analysis. The vestibular system operates closely with the reflexes to facilitate balance. Both the vestibular system and the reflex system are aligned to the visual system. Eye movements and visual perception skills are closely tied to the vestibular system. Impulses from the vestibular system affect the motor nerves that control eye movements. Children who don't develop good vestibular functioning are delayed in all gross motor patterns that require coordination of both sides of the body. (More than five ear infections during childhood can signal a vestibular dysfunction.) These children may also have difficulty maintaining posture with hand-eye coordination and fine motor control.

The vestibular system is very important in controlling breathing. In a study conducted at the University of Pittsburgh, researchers found a physical connection between the autonomic nervous system and the vestibular nuclei of the brain. When the vestibular system was stimulated, measurable changes were evident in heart rate, blood pressure, and the respiratory system.

## Learning Is Development

As discussed above, brain development and eye development occur from the same place. Eighteen days after conception, dimples develop in the center of the neural plate. These dimples come off the neural plate and eventually become the retinas of the eyes; retina and brain originate from the same place. Eye movements and REM (rapid eye movement) sleep occur when a fetus has an active mother. Sleep patterns are a good neurological indicator of a problem, as a measurement of one of the many internal rhythms of a child.

Feeling movement from the pregnant mother teaches the fetus how to adapt under a variety of gravity-based experiences. We call this the ability to learn about orientation-disorientation-reorientation. How well can the fetus recover from different balance experiences? Also, how fast can the fetus recover? This is a basis for learning "where I am in relationship to others in my world." Orientation gives the child a place to learn from, a perspective, so to speak. It teaches the fetus how to be flexible in its neurological patterning. This training helps later on.

## Vision and Learning

Vision is a dominant sense for learning. It is a guidance system that helps us move through our environment. The fetus, in its warm, dark, liquid environment, develops peripheral vision, which is critical for learning about orientation, balance, and, later, depth perception. Whether it is vision, hearing, movement, or sensing, there has to be a sequential progression from one stage to another; any stage being skipped or delayed has a profound effect on the fetus/baby/child/adult. Even the primitive survival reflexes need to be learned in a certain sequence.

What happens if a mother does not have a normal pregnancy? What happens if a mother is bedridden? The fetus is not able to experience and develop its own vestibular-balance system. What happens if a mother or fetus receives either no stimulation or excessive stimulation? For example, the American Academy of Pediatrics says that sharp, loud noises can affect the normal development of a fetus. The primitive reflexes may not begin to develop properly in utero to protect the fetus, those same reflexes may not inhibit on schedule, and learning difficulties may result.

## Fundamental Learning Skills

In our testing, it's important to check the balance of the eyes while open, with the child looking at a fixed target as a visual anchor. Can the child easily stand on one foot for a minute? Does he fall over or tense his muscles in order to stay balanced? Or does he lack the muscle strength to stand on one foot for one minute?

Having the child stand on one foot with the eyes closed challenges the child to draw upon his vestibular and kinesthetic ability to keep his balance. It also demonstrates whether the child can find his internal anchor point and maintain that focus.

Another test used to assess the balancing system of the child is the Vestibulo-Ocular Reflex (VOR). This reflex helps a person maintain a stable image on the retina by creating eye movements that offset corresponding head movements. The test is done in a darkened room. With eyes open, the child spins five times clockwise, five times counterclockwise, then stops.

The doctor shines a light toward the eyes looking for nystagmus (fast oscillating eye movements). If the nystagmus occurs for less than ten seconds, then the child has an underacting vestibulo-ocular reflex. If the nystagmus occurs for more than twenty seconds, then the child has an overacting vestibulo-ocular reflex. A nystagmus between ten and twenty seconds indicates a normal response. The VOR can be repeated by having the child spin while her eyes are closed.

Could some of the primitive reflexes previously discussed influence the vestibulo-ocular reflex and visual coordination? The answer is yes. As an infant turns his head to the side while on his back, his hand extends and provides a union of the eyes and hand. Next, conscious control comes into play, and finally the reflex is inhibited. Both asymmetrical and symmetrical tonic neck reflexes set the initial pattern of hand-eye coordination.

Some questions arise. What happens if the reflex does not become inhibited? How does that affect the control of the vestibular system with gross and fine motor development? Evidence suggests that a lack of inhibition of the primitive reflexes contributes to developmental delay in children and adults (to which AD/HD can be a part of the spectrum of disorders). When the primitive reflexes are not inhibited, it is like trying to walk down the street with a forty-pound backpack. This lack of inhibition will affect the vestibular function to help balance.

## Vestibular Function

One function of the vestibular system is apparent when a child has to copy from the board, when she turns her head to follow an object like a soccer ball, or even when she looks across a page. The vestibular system helps maintain normal muscle tone. Muscle strength is different than muscle tone. Tone helps us maintain our position (orientation), such as when an infant holds up his head. Or it could be how well we control our eye muscles. The vestibular system is very important for coordinating the three primary sensory systems that are sensitive to movement.

Body orientation is a basic skill a child needs to develop before she can begin to process more complicated cognitive functions in the brain.

## CASE HISTORY: School Readiness

Ben is an eight-year-old struggling with school. He cannot read or write very easily. And he has had some behavioral outbursts toward his classmates and teachers. Presently, Ben has been placed in a special education class.

When his school psychologist performed the Weschler Intelligence Scale Test for Children—a common IQ test given to assess learning potential—Ben scored 141 on the verbal IQ, 104 on the performance IQ, and 126 on the full scale IQ—all within the normal range. So the school psychologist recommended intensive reading and writing tutoring for Ben. This was a valid recommendation. However, Ben's parents wanted a second opinion and came to me for a developmental learning evaluation.

Before commencing an evaluation, I request that parents send me the results of all previous testing of their child in order to better understand what avenues the family has already taken to address their child's problem.

I assess the results of the Weschler by looking at the subtest scores to see if there is a difference of six or more between the low and the high. If that exists, then my experience tells me the child has a developmental delay. Ben's test results did show such a difference.

During Ben's evaluation I was especially interested in the level of his sensory-motor skills—tests not previously done. By performing those tests I found that Ben's balance, bilateral integration (both gross motor and fine motor skills), and his rhythm and timing were three

years below his chronological age. Although the earlier tutoring recommendation was valid and accurate for Ben, his parents and I
decided we would first address his basic skill deficiencies through a
developmental visual learning program, to give Ben the necessary
skills for the tutoring to be more effective. I have found that while
educational testing is valuable, working in a developmental motor
model, sequencing the activities through concrete skills first, will
make the tutoring and educational therapy more effective later on.

All the factors we have described contribute to determining
whether a child is ready for school. School readiness means that the
child's learning skills are able to match the demands placed upon her
in school. If the child's sensory-motor skills are not able to match
those demands, then the child makes adaptations and compensations
to try to complete the task. When the child still has difficulty meeting the demands, frustration and lack of motivation set in. This is
where behavioral problems such as AD/HD appear. The child is saying that the situation is too stressful for her to focus and concentrate.

Many children do not have the skills to be successful because they
are presented with the abstract, complex tasks like reading and writing while they are still working at a concrete, basic level. Failing is not
fun, and it can lead to a variety of emotional and behavioral problems.
Stress plays a large role in this equation. If a child is under constant,
prolonged stress, it begins to affect his biochemistry and the endocrine functions of his body. If a child is expending too much energy
trying to meet demands without the proper skill level needed to be
successful, one will see nutritional imbalances in his body.

## Development Is a Multifaceted Process

I have described, briefly, just some of the factors affecting behavioral
development and the development of intelligence. It's a vast and multifaceted subject, which makes it all the more important to look at
AD/HD in a holistic way. The belief that one drug or a series of drugs
can cure these conditions is plainly unrealistic. Though it's true that

the approach I advocate requires more time, more involvement, and, perhaps, more passion from parents, teachers, and doctors, when looking at the larger picture you see that the effort is worth it.

We have seen that prenatal and postnatal factors affect a child's development and potential. So, when we investigate AD/HD we must consider every aspect of the child, including the neurological, bio-chemical, physiological, psychological, and emotional. Trauma or illnesses, alcohol or drug abuse, even stress, can affect both prenatal and postnatal development, as these experiences can influence the organization and health of the nervous system.

## Caring for the Whole Child

Every child is special and unique. Each has a different learning style. Some simply lack the learning skill (sensory-motor processing abilities) to understand and execute a process on demand. Ritalin is very good at helping children conform to externally imposed rules. It makes children obedient. But giving a child Ritalin does not honor a child's uniqueness while helping her learn to function effectively within society.

A child's colds, sore throats, skinned knees, and even mumps are easily treated. However, when a child is diagnosed with AD/HD, dyslexia, and other developmental delays, finding the exact causes can be difficult. It can become even more perplexing when an obviously bright child has learning problems or when a child with devoted parents and a healthy home environment exhibits behavioral problems.

I believe the only truly effective method for treating this often baffling condition is the comprehensive, embracing holistic method outlined in the following chapters. I have seen drug therapy for AD/HD fail consistently, whereas the patients I have treated holistically have thrived.

# A Step-by-Step Guide to the Holistic Treatment of AD/HD

## There Is No Magic Bullet

The success stories of children in previous chapters of this book are inspiring. They offer great hope. But we must not be lulled into thinking that there is one simple holistic magic bullet for treating AD/HD.

AD/HD is a multifaceted disorder. According to Patricia S. Lemer, M.Ed., Researcher and Founder of the Developmental Delay Resources, AD/HD falls under a continuum of disorders that ranges from ADD, which is the least severe, and goes to AD/HD, LD (Learning Disability), PDD (Pervasive Developmental Disorder), and autism, which is the most severe.[1] Each child, or adult, has his own individual combination of symptoms and causes. Therefore, in order to treat the patient as a whole being, it is vital to first collect a detailed history. This information includes physical and/or birth trauma; lowered immune function, which may be caused by allergies, yeast infections, reactions to immunizations, overuse of antibiotics, and frequent illness; and congenital or other genetic problems.

## Step One: Incorporating a Holistic Philosophy

The holistic approach is to first identify the causes for the AD/HD behavior, then treat the reason for the imbalances that produce the symptoms, thus reducing or eliminating the symptoms.

To achieve this result, you will have to stop living out a doctor's diagnosis of AD/HD and no longer agree to accept traditional treatment of symptoms, which might include such approaches as counseling, special education, behavioral management, and medications.

By using the holistic approach, I find that alternative and complementary treatments do more than just treat symptoms. One of the pioneering doctors in this field of integrated medicine was Dr. Leo Galland. He believed that one must consider the total patient when determining treatment. This is done by taking a very detailed history that includes the effects of birth trauma, diet, environmental toxins and chemical sensitivities, allergic reactions, nutritional deficiencies, and human dynamics.

Jeffrey Bland, Ph.D., a leader in the field of nutrition and preventive health says we are in a state of "vertical ill health."[2] He means that people are not sick enough to lie down, even though they are unhealthy and out of balance with their own health. They derive some benefit from prescription drugs, but then they struggle with all the side effects from those same medications.

Although there are a wide variety of holistic treatments available, I follow some consistent guidelines when developing a treatment plan. It is critically important to help empower the family, including the child, to accept at least part of the task of recovery and health maintenance. Next, there needs to be an emphasis on sound nutrition, which includes a detoxification program along with better digestive absorption. Third, I recommend finding ways to reduce stress, get exercise, proper rest, sleep, and emotional health. It is important to improve all relationships. These factors are all part of embracing the holistic philosophy.

## Step Two: Cleaning Up the Toxins

Having embraced Step One, a holistic philosophy, the next step is to clean up the toxins that may exist in the body. Our food, air, and water are more polluted than ever before. If your child attends school, most likely she is under a great deal of stress. Today the pressure placed on children to achieve, succeed, and compete is nearly insurmountable. When children are under constant stress and not performing to their full potential, their immune system (the body's defense system) gets worn down. This pattern can cause a child to become more susceptible to toxins, such as heavy metals, radiation, pesticides, and so on, which affect the brain, attention, concentration, and behavior. A weakened immune system can also affect the digestive tract, respiratory function, as well as the brain and processing systems, which affect memory, concentration, and motor skills.

When we think of brain and processing problems, there are two types: those related to an immune system breakdown and those related to detoxification problems. Children with an immune-system problem exhibit the following symptoms:[3]

- Allergies
- Frequent ear infections
- Sinus and strep infections
- Respiratory problems such as bronchitis and asthma
- Poor skin color or eczema
- Digestive problems, which include diarrhea, reflux, or constipation
- Dark circles under the eyes, red ears, or apple cheeks
- History of immunization reactions
- Decline in development from 18 to 30 months
- Chronic unexplained fevers
- Yeast infections

Children with detoxification problems exhibit the following symptoms:[4]

- Agitated sleep
- Wild swings in mood and function
- Hyperactivity
- High consumption of apple juice
- Sensitivity to dyes, chemicals, perfumes, or medications
- Self-injurious or violent behaviors

There are very sophisticated blood, urine, and stool tests that pinpoint what is occurring within the immune system, digestive system, respiratory system, and detoxification pathways. These tests can measure responses to gluten and casein sensitivity (as in allergies); the presence of yeast metabolites or intestinal parasites; toxic metals such as lead, cadmium, mercury, and aluminum; and amino acid imbalances. Although these tests can be expensive, they are definitely helpful. In many cases I have found that allergic reactions can be either delayed or triggered when one food is combined with another food. I believe that some allergic reactions are the body's signal to limit the intake of or exposure to the foreign substance or toxin.

There are two ways to improve the immune system and improve the detoxification pathways: reduce the toxic burden by removing some of what is ingested and add nutritional supplementation. Jeffrey Bland, Ph.D., in *The 20-Day Rejuvenation Diet Program*, found that the body's detoxification pathways require heavy nutritional support every step of the way.[5] Fasting should not be done because it inhibits the detoxification process by shutting down the liver enzymes necessary to clear toxins from the body and transform them into harmless compounds.

## Step Three: Refueling

After the body has been detoxed, it must be refueled with real or clean foods, vitamins, minerals, and supplements. It is critically important to eliminate additives, food colors, artificial flavors, and salicylates. Next, I recommend consuming a dairy- and wheat-free diet if casein and gluten allergies showed up in the preliminary tests or are suspected. During the refueling process, a yeast, mold, and sugar-free diet is best along with nutritional supplementation, including filtered water, vitamins and minerals, essential fatty acids, and amino acids.

## Step Four: Utilizing Effective Complementary Treatments

I have found the following to be effective treatments for AD/HD: homeopathy, cell salts, essential oils, sensory-motor integration (which includes vision therapy), osteopathic manipulation, and auditory integration training.

Chapter 9 includes a description of the use of homeopathy, cell salts, and essential oils to improve mental clarity and focus without the use of medications. In addition, activities and exercises are introduced that are necessary to help improve the sensory-motor systems (visual, vestibular, speech/language, auditory, and kinesthetic) that affect the skills of movement, balance, rhythm/timing, and bilateral integration, all of which are crucial for optimal learning and academic achievement.

When these skills are not fully developed to match the demands placed upon children in school, learning, behavior, and attention problems will occur. These problems are often labeled AD/HD and, according to the medical and pharmaceutical establishment, are suitable for drug treatment. Thus, the terrible cycle continues.

Let's see how our biochemistry affects learning and development.

# Cleaning Up the Inner Environment

These startling statistics about chemicals affecting our world, our health, and the health of our children are only a glimpse of the overall picture:

- More than half of U.S. cities have levels of air pollution that exceed federal standards.
- A recent report by the Environmental Protection Agency revealed that toxic pollution dumped into the environment in 1998 was three times higher than previous estimates: a staggering 7.3 billion pounds.
- A new study from Stanford Medical School indicates that exposure to home-use pesticides can cause brain damage.
- According to *U.S. News and World Report,* reported cases of autism in California rose 210 percent. In New York, the number of children with learning disabilities jumped 55 percent between 1983 and 1996. These trends have

forced the Environmental Protection Agency to ban the popular pesticide Dursban because of its risk to children.[1]

We have used technology to create our world without being fully aware of the laws of nature. We have damaged certain areas of our ecosystem to overdevelop other areas. As a result, our water, air, and food contain more environmental toxins than ever before. When our food, for example, comes from polluted sources, we are consuming fuel that depletes our energy and well-being. As our bodies become weaker, we become more susceptible to attacks from organisms foreign to our bodies.

Environmental toxins from the air, water, and food can accumulate in the body if the immune system is unable to help release these toxins. Many children with AD/HD have weakened immune systems because their bodies must work harder to compensate for their deficiencies.

## Managing Our Food Artificially

In the early 1900s the business practice of adding man-made chemicals to food began for three reasons: to increase food production, to kill unwanted grasses and insects, and to manage food supplies for preservation. However, in the process of destroying pests in our food supplies, ranging from crops to livestock, the natural balance of the ecosystem was forever disturbed. Since we have manipulated food by artificial means, our bodies have had a difficult time assimilating what is unnatural.

### Pesticides in Our Crops

Pesticides, for example, have a negative effect on learning and sensory-motor abilities. In 1998, Elizabeth Guillette, from the University of Arizona, headed up a team of scientists from the Technical Institute of Sonora, Mexico, which studied the effects of pesticides on brain function in school-age children. The study included thirty-three preschool children living in a valley in Mexico where pesticides were regularly used by farmers. Also included in the study were seventeen other preschool children who lived in the foothills, where pesticides were not used. The situation set up a perfect control group and test group. Each group was tested using gross and fine motor skills, memory, and drawing ability. The results showed that the group of children living in the farming community that used pesticides scored much lower on the testing than did the group of children not exposed to pesticides.[2]

David Carpenter, a neurotoxicologist from Albany, New York, reviewed the results and became concerned because the level of pesticides the Mexican children were exposed to was equal to the amount of pesticides found in many places in the United States. He also noticed that the Mexican children routinely exposed to pesticides showed no symptoms except that they had brain-processing problems.

If the children who participated in this study showed no overt signs and symptoms, then could the pesticides that affected them be an underlying cause of learning and developmental problems in all children who are exposed to such levels? This study, which was reported in *Environmental Health Perspectives*, clearly connects pesticide poisoning to difficulties with cognitive processing.

The Environmental Working Group, a nonprofit research group based in Washington, D.C., did another study in 1998. The results showed that one million children five years old and younger living in the United States are exposed to high levels of pesticides found in fruits, vegetables, and commercial baby food. The group found high levels of organophosphates (a common agricultural pesticide) in 80,000 samples of food. Organophosphates inhibit an enzyme in the body that helps regulate the body's nervous system. This particular pesticide can be very harmful to the neurological system of the developing child because a young child's developing brain does not yet have the protective mechanisms to deal with contaminants.

This exposes infants and neonates to a greater risk of permanent brain and neurological damage, which can affect motor and cognitive skills.

The developing fetus is also at higher risk for developmental problems if the mother is exposed to chemical toxins. Although the mother may not be harmed, these toxins can become concentrated in her placenta and pass to the fetus, affecting her unborn child. Researchers at the State University of New York, Oswego, found that babies with moderate amounts of PCPs in their umbilical chords performed more poorly than unexposed babies in tests assessing visual recognition of faces, ability to shut out distractions, and overall intelligence.

## Pesticides in Our Livestock

One of our biggest food-source problems exists when animals are given feed containing pesticides, which are absorbed and stored in their tissues. Ranchers also dip and spray these animals with extremely toxic compounds, and some animals are given high doses of toxic drugs. In addition, many of these animals receive hormones and antibiotics that are dangerous for humans. The EPA has found that animals containing these toxins and poisons are a major source of pesticides found in human diets. It is very important to eat organically raised meat, which is free of pesticides and chemicals.

## Pesticides in Our Soil

The soil in which food is grown also has a profound impact on the food's quality. Since our soil has been modified and manipulated, our food has fewer nutrients. Our agricultural techniques have also robbed our soil of its important trace minerals, leaving it depleted and filled with pesticides and other dangerous chemicals. Pesticide use is for profit, not for health. Our bodies are not made to withstand the chemicals in our soil and food. Perhaps the fact that we are seeing more degenerative human health conditions than ever before shows a correlation between the breakdown of our bodies and the deterioration of the soil in which our food is grown.

## Pesticides in Our Homes

Home is the most common place for us to be exposed to pesticides. Consider the products we use: insect sprays for houseplants and to control termites and cockroaches, flea collars on pets, and pesticides to control insects in the garden. Even the peelings on fresh fruits and vegetables may be a source of insecticides. Tap water often contains chemicals, as well as contaminants that filtration systems cannot remove. And there is a growing body of evidence pointing to compounds called neurotoxicants, which may contribute to increased learning disorders and developmental delays in children. Neurotoxicants have been found in substances as varied as tuna, lawn sprays, vaccines, and head lice shampoo.

When fetuses are exposed to chemicals during their developmental period, scientists now believe it creates increased risk for autism, dyslexia, learning disabilities, and AD/HD. A new study from the National Academy of Sciences suggests that a combination of neurotoxicants and genes may account for almost 25 percent of all learning problems.[3]

## Heavy Metal Toxicity

Heavy metal toxicity is another problem. Hair mineral analysis is an easy, inexpensive method to measure metal toxicities in the body. Studies conducted within the criminal population of the United States found high levels of cadmium and lead. Could there be a link between violent behavior and brain chemistry being altered by these metals? Poor nutrition and heavy metals seem to go together.

## Lead

In a study conducted in 1996, over three million children (12 percent of the U.S. population) were found to have 10 micrograms per deciliter or higher of lead in their bodies.[4] The Centers for Disease Control (CDC) is so concerned about lead toxicity and exposure that it has changed its safe level from 3 micrograms to 10 micrograms.[5] Our lead levels seem to be increasing. A group of scientists compared ancient bone samples of pre-Incan Peruvians (prior to 500 B.C.E.) to today's humans and found that we currently have over five hundred times more lead in our systems. Another study indicated that 400,000 babies with toxic blood levels are delivered each year in the United States.[6]

Children seem to be more susceptible to lead poisoning than adults due to their smaller size and the fact that most of the lead in children's bodies is stored in their brain. In addition, it is harder for children to detoxify the lead from their bodies. If a fetus is exposed to lead while in the womb, its brain development and nervous system can be affected much more than an older child or adult, because the unborn child is undergoing intensive growth and development during the gestation period.

Studies have shown that pregnant mothers who smoke routinely expose the fetus to lead and other heavy metal toxicities. Adults in general absorb about 15 percent, which reaches the digestive tract, while pregnant mothers and their babies can absorb up to 50 percent.[7]

Lead poisoning is reaching such epidemic proportions that at an annual meeting of the American Academy of Child and Adolescent Psychiatry, Dr. Herbert Needleman said that a child with learning problems or behavioral disorders should be tested for lead exposure.

High levels of lead may also be found in drinking water. The EPA discovered over eight hundred city water systems, which served over thirty million people, with lead levels beyond federal standards. Drinking water is second only to lead paint as a source of lead poisoning. Lead can be absorbed from old lead pipes or from new brass fixtures. And lead can be leeched from hollow ware (coffee mugs) into the liquids they hold, especially hot acidic beverages.[8] Other common sources of lead include paint in old houses, imported dishware, and lead in the air, soil, and table water of highly industrialized areas. Sludge, which is used to fertilize crops, also introduces lead into the soil.

Some of the behavioral characteristics found in children suffering from high levels of lead include hyperactivity, learning disabilities, temper tantrums, withdrawal, fearfulness, and other emotional problems. Sensory-motor functions, such as vision, hearing, balance, poor memory, and academic problems, may also be characteristic. Clearly, children with lead toxicity have problems with focus, attention, and cognitive function.

Lead reduces the levels of calcium in the body, which is important for brain cells to transfer information between neurons. Other trace minerals, which are depleted by lead toxicity but are necessary for processing information, are copper, zinc, iron, and manganese.

Robert Tuthill, Ph.D., of the University of Massachusetts, Amherst, conducted an interesting study concerning the correlation between AD/HD and lead toxicity. Lead toxicity tests were performed on 227 first-grade students. These same students were also evaluated for AD/HD by using a questionnaire filled out by physicians, nurses, and teachers. The results indicated that children who were diagnosed with AD/HD had higher lead levels.[9]

## Aluminum

This heavy metal can be another cause of behavioral problems and attention difficulties. Aluminum affects the brain and nervous system. Sources of aluminum are from cooking food in aluminum pots and pans, drinking soda from aluminum cans, aluminum foil, and airborne aluminum in highly industrialized areas. Low calcium and magnesium levels increase aluminum toxicity in the body.

## Cadmium

Cadmium, a highly toxic heavy metal stored in the liver, kidneys, and blood, affects a fetus's ability to absorb zinc. Some studies suggest that high levels of cadmium correlate with low zinc levels and that children showing such a profile have more learning problems.

The major sources of cadmium poisoning are cigarettes, coffee, and refined white flour. If cadmium is swallowed, only a small amount is absorbed into the body, but if it is breathed in through the air, about 50 percent of it is absorbed. (Fortunately, there are methods available to reduce the cadmium that companies release into the air.)

There is a strong connection between high levels of cadmium and our diets. In a study testing for cadmium levels in the hair of 150 schoolchildren, those with toxic cadmium levels ate a diet high in refined carbohydrates.[10] Cadmium replaces zinc in its biochemical reactions in the body, slowing down body processes normally requiring zinc.

## Copper

Copper is another toxic metal that can be readily passed from mother to fetus through the placenta. Low levels of zinc enhance copper levels in the body. Because zinc helps balance emotions, low zinc levels and high copper levels can be a frequent cause of hyperactivity, learning problems, and recurrent infections. Stress is a big factor in the depletion of zinc. When we are under stress, our adrenals overwork and can produce a copper-binding protein. Copper may be absorbed into the body from swimming pools, drinking water, and from copper water pipes.

## Mercury

Aside from cadmium, mercury is one of the most toxic heavy metals. Exposure to mercury can begin as early as in the womb. The fetus is ten times more sensitive than an adult to mercury toxicity. In a study conducted by Deborah Rice for Health Canada, monkeys showing even very low levels of mercury poisoning exhibited behaviors of impulsivity and distractibility, and they couldn't learn.

Mercury amalgams (fillings in our teeth) are one cause of mercury toxicity and chronic illness. Other sources of mercury include drinking water, bleached flour, processed foods, fabric softeners, wood preservatives, pesticides, and fertilizers. Some symptoms of mercury poisoning include dizziness, loss of memory, irritability, muscle weakness, headaches, fatigue, and skin inflammation.

## Testing for Biochemical Imbalances

Some biochemical imbalances in the body can be detected by hair analysis, which measures mineral content of the hair. This measurement reflects the mineral content of the body's tissue, which is important to know because many mineral imbalances of the body signal metabolic imbalances before any symptoms are evident.

Minerals act as "spark plugs" of the body. They are used for many enzyme reactions within the body. Dr. Paul C. Eck of Analytical Research Labs, based in Phoenix, has researched hair trace-mineral analysis for over twelve years. His studies conclude that many chemical imbalances actually create stress within the body. This stress response can be a major factor in AD/HD behaviors.

Dr. Eck has identified five major types of biochemical imbalances that cause learning disabilities, hyperactivity, and other behavior-related problems:

1. Elevated toxic metals
2. Copper imbalance
3. Overactivity of the adrenal glands
4. Exhaustion of the adrenal glands
5. Mineral deficiencies/imbalances

Mineral analysis looks at ratios of different minerals as a way to assess the biochemical balance of the body. Out-of-balance ratios of sodium and potassium, for example, can cause increased excitability and irritability. Children may be violent or aggressive. Some have difficulty with sleep patterns.

Ritalin has a calming effect on some hyperactive children because it seems to raise the level of adrenal gland secretions, which in turn raises the child's sodium level, but also raises her blood pressure. But adrenal function can be enhanced by naturally balancing a child's sodium-potassium levels through her food intake, enabling the child to better handle stress and relax.

## Calcium

Calcium is one of the most important building blocks in the body. Many children have low calcium levels even though their diets are full of milk, cheese, and other sources of calcium. Excessive salt intake can deplete the body of sedative minerals such as calcium, magnesium, and zinc. Low levels of these minerals can contribute to hyperactive behavior.

## Phosphorus

Many times high phosphorus levels occur in conjunction with low calcium and magnesium levels. This can cause a child to be more susceptible to seizures and become hyperactive. Carbonated drinks and red meat are high in phosphorus and need to be reduced.

## Iron

The *American Journal of Diseases in Childhood* reported in 1992 that iron deficiency is the most common nutritional disorder of children. Low iron levels lead to decreased attention and persistence for completing a task. A study conducted on females sixteen and seventeen years of age who took iron supplements showed a marked improvement in their concentration, energy, and mood. Iron deficiency, which causes anemia, also needs to be brought back into balance because children with an iron deficiency are more apt to absorb lead.

## Zinc

Low zinc levels have been linked to hyperactive behavior. Because zinc is a sedative mineral, it helps to relax the nervous system.

## Therapeutic Baths

Therapeutic baths can be very effective to help release heavy metals and other toxins through the skin. I have found the following bath formulas—which were invented by Dr. Hazel Parcells and are discussed at length in the book by Joseph Dispenza, *Live Better Longer: The Parcells Center 7-Step Plan for Health and Longevity*—to be very helpful in throwing off toxins.

## Formula One

*When to do it:* If you have been exposed to environmental radiation or X rays. Air travel, for instance, will greatly increase levels of radiation in our bodies; even simple dental X rays will leave deposits in the body that will interfere with healthy functioning.

*Indications:* General muscle aches, mild nausea, more fatigue than usual, headaches, slight dizziness, discomforts associated with jet lag, or a disturbance in balance.

*How to do it:* Dissolve 1 pound of sea salt or rock salt and 1 pound of baking soda in a tub of water as hot as can be tolerated. While soaking in the bath, sip a mixture of ½ teaspoon rock salt and ½ teaspoon baking soda in a glass of warm water. Remain in the bath until the water has cooled. Do not shower for at least four hours following the bath.

## Formula Two

*When to do it:* If you have been exposed to heavy metals, such as aluminum, or to carbon monoxide or unburned carbons, pesticide sprays, or toxins. Cooking with aluminum will bring on symptoms. Frequent commuters absorb carbon monoxide through their skin into their body. Eating food that has not been cleaned of pesticides can lead to accumulations of pesticides in the cells of the body.

*Indications:* A general feeling of being "out of sorts," decreased energy, upper respiratory discomfort, a shortness of breath, light-headedness, or impaired balance.

*How to do it:* Add 1 cup regular brand Clorox bleach (with the blue and white label) to a tub of water as hot as can be tolerated. Remain in the bath until the water has cooled. Do not shower for at least four hours following the bath.

**Note:** When people read a recommendation like this—that they should actually allow bleach to touch their skin—their eyebrows go up. Rest assured, the amount of bleach recommended here, combined with this much water, cannot hurt you. In fact, it can and will remove toxins with utmost effectiveness because it is a powerful oxygenator. You'll feel the difference in a matter of hours.

Be sensible, of course. Don't use more bleach than is recommended. But do be adventurous. Try it!

## Vaccinations

There is a growing controversy concerning the safety of vaccinations. One of the major concerns comes from a study conducted in 1998 by Andrew Wakefield and his colleagues, who reported that the measles-mumps-rubella (MMR) vaccine might contribute to autism.[11] Medical groups, the media, even the U.S. Congress are calling for more investigation into the possible risks associated with vaccinations. Here are some of the political developments concerning the use of vaccinations:[12]

- Federal health officials called for immediate suspension of the rotovirus vaccine after it was linked to a potentially fatal form of bowel blockage called intussusception.
- U.S. Representative Dan Burton, himself the grandfather of a child who developed autism shortly after receiving a diptheria-pertussis-tetanus (DPT) shot, held a congressional hearing on vaccine safety.
- The Association of American Physicians and Surgeons called for a nationwide moratorium on mandatory vaccinations, in particular the hepatitis B (HiB) vaccine. "The Association is deeply concerned," it said, "that Federal vaccine policy results in the violation of informed consent, and is based on incomplete studies of efficacy and potential adverse effects of vaccines." The group was strongly critical of school districts that require vaccinations in order for children to attend school, saying, "Parents may give 'consent' to the vaccine under duress."
- The Food and Drug Administration called on vaccine manufacturers to phase out vaccines containing the mercury-based preservative thimerosal. Considering the large number of vaccinations given to infants, it is possible for babies to accumulate enough thimerosal in their systems to approach federal limits on exposure to mercury.
- Researchers reported in the *Archives of Disease in Childhood* that premature infants may be at increased risk of life-threatening apnea (the temporary cessation of breathing) following DPT and HiB vaccinations.

- Barbara Loe Fisher of the National Vaccine Information Center asks the question, "Why are immune and neurological diseases on the rise?" This would include diabetes, asthma, multiple sclerosis, autism, and learning disabilities. Public health, she says, is not only measured by the absence of disease but also by the prevalence of chronic disease. She also says that we are suppressing infectious disease because of the number of vaccinations a child receives before first grade. How does this affect public health?

There is a link between vaccines and autism. Why? The key to this link is in researching the timing, administration, and grouping of vaccinations.

Perhaps parents should be given the right of informed consent, the right to fully accept or reject vaccines for their children. There should be full and uncensored disclosure, as there is on the insert of almost every over-the-counter or prescribed medication, detailing the benefits and possible side effects of every vaccine before it is administered. Parents need to read about immunizations and become better educated about which vaccinations are really necessary and which are unnecessary. I also believe we may be vaccinating our babies too young. These are major health issues of our times.

One interesting research study of pregnant women showed that the incidence of brain tumors in children of Salk-vaccinated mothers is thirteen times greater than children of mothers who had not received the Salk vaccine—a polio vaccination developed by Dr. Jonas Salk.

But vaccines are big business. Revenues worldwide amount to about $3 billion, and that figure will more than double in five years. In the United States the revenue from vaccines is nearly $1 billion, up from $500 million in 1990, an increase of 100 percent over ten years.[13]

One question parents often ask is: Why do their young children need a hepatitis B vaccine when hepatitis B is often a sexually transmitted disease? The three recommended doses of the hepatitis B vaccination cost more than $40. If you multiply that amount by the number of children receiving the HiB vaccine, you can see how much that one vaccination contributes to drug companies' profits.

## Absorption and Assimilation of Nutrients Are the Keys

It is not what you eat, but what your body does with what you eat, that is important. Many children with developmental delays or learning problems don't have enough fuel to power themselves efficiently. A child must be able to call on her energy reserves to be successful in learning and development. And so even before a developmental-learning program begins, a child's absorption and assimilation abilities must be improved.

### Candida

*Candida albicans* is a yeast that grows naturally in the intestinal tract. The normal flora (bacteria) in our gut is important to help break down the food we eat. But if we are under stress, consume a great deal of simple sugars or fruit juices, and/or have taken a great deal of antibiotics, the yeast in our intestines can multiply to the point that it becomes out of balance. Excessive yeast growth can cause learning or behavioral problems.

Many children who suffer with either chronic ear infections (more than five) or upper respiratory infections and have used multiple rounds of antibiotics have a greater susceptibility to yeast infection because the antibiotic can kill good bacteria in the intestinal tract, just as it can kill bad bacteria in the body.

Candida loves sugar and simple carbohydrates. *Yeast and How They Can Make You Sick*, written by William G. Crook, M.D., has helped many children diagnosed with AD/HD. He says that candida releases toxins into the body and can weaken the immune system. Some symptoms of candida include bloating, constipation, diarrhea, colic, cramps, nausea, ear infections, respiratory infections, asthma, sinus infections, eczema and skin rashes, sleeping problems, hyperactivity, irritability, short attention span, impulsivity, memory problems, mood swings, depression, sugar cravings, runny nose, allergies to chemical substances, urinary problems, and bladder infections.

## Diagnosis of Candida

Many tests are not reliable for detecting candida. Even a high amount of candida in the stool may not be a true diagnostic indicator. In fact, Leo Galland, M.D., found that if candida is found to be positive in the stool it is *less* likely to be successfully treated by using antifungal medication than if it is found to be negative. The best way to diagnose candida is by using a yeast questionnaire, a physical examination, and a medical history.

Candida causes what is called a "leaky gut," where food allergens are easily absorbed by the body. Foods that encourage yeast to grow out of control are chocolate, pizza, fruit juices, refined carbohydrates, and alcoholic beverages. An overabundance of yeast causes cravings for fermented, pickled, or smoked foods. Taking *Lactobacillus acidophilus*, *Lactobacillus bifidus*, and *Lactobacillus bulgaricus* on an empty stomach can replenish the beneficial bacteria in the intestines.

Garlic is a natural antifungal product that can be used to reduce candida. Taking certain herbs that kill the yeast can also be effective. Such herb formulas include probiotics, aged garlic extract, caprylic acid, citrus seed extract, and oil of oregano. Herbal cleanses can also be used to detoxify the intestines and move the bowels more regularly, creating a positive environment for good flora to grow. But detoxing without replenishing the body with beneficial bacteria and nutrition is not effective. And antibiotics and immune-suppressant drugs, such as steroids, should be discontinued if possible during this process. If you need to take an antibiotic, supplement with *Lactobacillus acidophilus* or *Lactobacillus bifidus* for at least one month after you discontinue use of the antibiotic.

Some other food and nutrient malabsorption problems, which may respond to detoxification, are parasites and food sensitivities. However, any detoxification program needs to be supervised by a trained health practitioner.

## Ear Infections and AD/HD

Ear infections are a red flag of possible developmental problems. A study reported in *Clinical Pediatrics* by Dr. Randi Hagerman and Alice Falkenstein found an association between recurrent otitis media (ear infections) and later hyperactivity. Sixty-seven children ranging from six to thirteen years old were studied. All demonstrated specific school learning problems; some had been diagnosed with AD/HD, and some among them were taking stimulant medications.

The results of the study showed that 94 percent of the children medicated for hyperactivity had three or more ear infections during their life; 69 percent had more than ten. Of the nonmedicated children with learning problems, 50 percent had three or more ear infections during their life; 20 percent had more than ten. Of all the children in the study, 79 percent had more than ten ear infections before one year of age.[14]

In a collaborative study of 2,565 children in Boston, more than two-thirds had at least one ear infection by age three, and one-third had at least three ear infections. Ear infections are one of the most common childhood illnesses.

### Food Allergies and Ear Infections

Otitis media is a chronic inflammatory disease of the mucoperiosteal lining of the eustachian tube, middle ear, and mastoid air cells. Recurrent accumulation of fluid behind the tympanic membrane leads to, among other things, a possible hearing impairment.[15] In one interesting study, 81 out of 104 patients (78 percent) who showed symp-

toms of food allergies also had recurrent serious otitis media. An elimination diet resulted in a significant reduction of the ear infections
(86 percent), while a challenge diet—deliberately including suspected
offending foods—provoked a recurrence of ear infections in 94 percent of the cases.[16]

With chronic ear infections, fluid will collect in the ears. To understand how this feels, put cotton in your ears and try to have a con-
versation with someone. After a while you probably withdraw because
everything you hear is garbled. When a child has chronic fluid in his
ears, he doesn't have the opportunity to learn how to use his ears.
These children are at higher risk to become developmentally delayed
in language and speech. They may also have difficulty following directions. Chronic ear infections also affect balance and orientation. If
balance is poor, it can affect eye movements, which are directly related
to reading and writing. A child suffering a developmentally delayed
ear-eye problem might skip words, lose her place, or reread pages of
a book constantly. This setup could contribute to AD/HD behaviors.

The time to watch for ear infections in infants is from six to twelve
months, when they are getting off formula and dairy products and
other foods are being introduced. This is when ear infections start.
After age two, ear infections become less frequent as the spaces
between the canals of the ears get bigger, enabling mucous to drain
to the back of the throat, which may cause strep throat, or drain down
the front, causing a runny, stuffy nose all winter. Some other symptoms, which include red cheeks, red ears, and circles under the eyes,
are all symptoms of allergies.

I recommend staying off milk, cheese, yogurt, ice cream, and pud-
ding and staying on a casein-free diet for at least two months.

## The Overuse of Antibiotics

If a child suffers more than ten ear infections from infancy to three
years of age and the predominant method of treatment is antibiotics,
the child has a greater chance of developing AD/HD or other learning

and behavioral problems. Antibiotic usage is on the rise. In 1994 there were 281 million prescriptions written for antibiotics—that's half of all prescriptions written. The American Pediatric Association says the prescribing of antibiotics needs to slow down. Here are some suggestions concerning antibiotics:

- Understand that when antibiotics are taken they not only kill the bad bacteria in our bodies, but the beneficial bacteria as well. Each of us should have two to five pounds of beneficial bacteria to protect us from negative influences in the environment. When beneficial bacteria cannot protect a child's body, the child's behavior, learning, and concentration will be affected.
- If you are taking antibiotics more than two to four times a winter, ask your doctor if there are any other options. Because of overuse of antibiotics, our bodies are now breeding bacteria that are resistant to those antibiotics.
- Eat organic meats whenever possible. Fifty-five percent of all the antibiotics used in the United States are fed to livestock. Therefore, the dairy foods and animal products we eat may be laced with antibiotics.

## Sugar and Hyperactivity

What is the relationship between sugar and hyperactivity? A number of medical studies suggest that there is no relationship between sugar and behavior, but I disagree. Their findings were inconsistent because the studies contained numerous flaws. Many different forms of sugars were used. In some studies sugar was given on an empty stomach, and sometimes on a full stomach; when a child is sensitive to other foods this can alter the results.

The truth is that hypoglycemia (low blood sugar) is one of the most important causes of hyperactivity. In 1973, Dr. Benjamin Feingold, a California allergist, discovered in his practice that over half of his hyperactive patients improved once they eliminated salicylate foods, artificial colors, flavors, and preservatives. Dr. Feingold also found that sugar made hyperactivity worse.

Children have difficulty handling sugar, especially in foods classified as refined carbohydrates. A study concerning the link between sugar and hyperactivity, conducted at the New York Institute of Child Development, showed that of 265 children tested, 74 percent did not have the ability to digest sugar and refined carbohydrates. When the children were put on a diet consisting of foods that promote stable blood sugar levels, their hyperactivity was gone after three weeks.[17]

How does sugar affect hyperactivity? The brain needs glucose (sugar) to function. If glucose weren't present in the brain, we would fall into a coma. When glucose levels in the brain or bloodstream are low, the adrenal glands produce a hormone called epinephrine. Epinephrine, also known as adrenaline, profoundly affects just about every gland, organ, and system of the body. When we are under stress our body's "fight or flight" response kicks in, releasing adrenaline, which affects the entire biochemistry of the body. It can affect moods, behaviors, and learning. Children whose bodies are constantly releasing adrenaline as a way to combat stress will have dilated pupils, poor focusing, reduced peripheral vision, irritability, and poor concentration.

What we eat or do not eat can also trigger adrenaline. Eating the wrong foods creates stress in the body because the body's biochemistry tries to compensate for itself. When hypoglycemia exists, there is not enough glucose in the bloodstream. Not eating frequently enough can make it difficult for the body to maintain stable glucose levels. Another cause for hypoglycemia is eating too much refined sugar or carbohydrates. When the body cannot metabolize all the sugar eaten, it thinks glucose levels in the blood are too low. In this condition, called reactive hypoglycemia, the pancreas releases insulin into the bloodstream to stabilize blood glucose levels; but when too much sugar is eaten, the pancreas believes there is already enough glucose and so it does not produce enough insulin. Once the consumed sugar is used up, the body "panics" because glucose levels fall, and adrenaline is released, which affects behavior.

A study conducted at Yale University assessed whether children reacted more strongly than adults to sugar consumption. Blood sugar levels were measured every half hour for five hours. When these levels remain in the normal range, it indicates that adrenaline is doing its job. However, after eating sugar, the children's adrenaline levels were ten times higher than adults and remained higher five hours longer. Every child in the study exhibited symptoms from the increased adrenaline in their bloodstreams, whereas only one adult had symptoms. The study concluded that children had more sensitivity to sugar than adults.[18]

Sugar can be addictive. It depletes our body of protein, calcium, and trace minerals, such as chromium. Low chromium causes myopia (an inability to see things far away). Sugar also depletes our body of vitamin B complex, which can cause the beneficial bacteria in the intestinal tract to become depleted. This negatively affects the immune system. Sugar can cause hyperactivity, poor concentration, and nervousness. And sugar is hidden in many foods. Check the labels. It is often found in ketchup, french fries, hot dogs, salad dressings, baby foods, and even in iodized salt and peanut butter.

Besides sugar, another factor to consider is the ratio of proteins to carbohydrates. Refined carbohydrates include glucose, sucrose, milk fructose, and corn syrup. Complex carbohydrates include whole grains, pastas, and vegetables. Bonnie Spring, Ph.D., a researcher at Texas Tech University, found that children who ate a high carbohydrate breakfast scored lower on attention tests than children who did not eat any breakfast at all.[19] When a child eats a high carbohydrate breakfast, the effects on brain function begin thirty minutes after the meal and can last the entire morning. If a child eats a sugary or high carbohydrate lunch, the effects can last the entire day.

Carbohydrates make us sleepy. Protein gives us energy. Protein contains crucial amino acids, essential for building muscles, organs, glands, and other tissues of the body. Amino acids help the brain make connections, called neurotransmitters. Children suffering with food sensitivities and allergies may have difficulty digesting protein, and therefore their bodies may not be assimilating these essential amino acids.

What foods can we eat that will give us the most energy and stimulate our learning and development? Read on to find out.

# Feed the Body, Feed the Mind

If your pediatrician says your child's eating habits are okay but you are doubtful, eat exactly what your child eats for one week. After that week ask yourself how you feel. That might mean you will be eating goldfish crackers, sugarcoated breakfast cereals, and brightly colored beverages right alongside your child. If that seems too harsh for you, then another approach would be to observe your child's behavior based on what he is eating. Watch for foods your child craves. These foods most likely are causing an addictive reaction. Sometimes parents need to become detectives to determine how their child's diet might be affecting his behavior.

How much does our diet affect our health? Medical researchers have made a connection between diet and many forms of chronic diseases, such as asthma, arthritis, diabetes, heart disease, and cancer. We eat too much processed food, such as fast foods, which contain fat and additives, and meat laced with growth hormones and antibiotics. In fact, some studies indicate that about five million pounds of antibiotics and hormones are used each year to encourage higher production of milk in cows and to make animals grow faster.

As of June 1998, the Food and Drug Administration had approved over 2,800 food additives.[1] I contend that many of these additives are causing food allergies in children and leading to their poor behavior, which is then characterized as AD/HD. Remember: Allergies are a result of the body defending itself against foreign elements.

## Signs of Food Allergies

Two things can occur when we develop food allergies. Undigested food moves into the bloodstream, where the cells react to these particles. Or the food interacts directly with the organs of the body, causing a negative reaction. When the body comes into contact with these irritants (allergens), it attempts in various ways to destroy them. White blood cells (infection fighters) may be produced, or immune proteins may be elevated. Both these signs can easily be found in a simple blood test.

Some symptoms include inflammation, tissue swelling, burning, sneezing, and rashes. Other common symptoms we may see are headaches, fatigue or drowsiness, poor concentration, short attention span, hyperactivity, or irritability. Some physical observations include dark circles under the eyes (allergy shiners) accentuated by puffiness under the eyes, which is caused by fluid retention in the tissues. This fluid retention can occur in the brain as well. The whites of the eyes may look pinkish or red from dilated blood vessels. Food allergies can cause muscle aches, digestive symptoms such as bloating or gas, difficulty breathing, and skin pallor. Some other symptoms include dry itchy skin, eczema, or bumpy areas on the legs, arms, or face. We have also seen in children with food allergies a chronic stuffy nose, sinus congestion, halitosis (bad breath), and asthma. These children might complain of stomachaches, indigestion, and constipation. It is estimated that 25 to 30 million people suffer from allergies that affect their health.[2]

## Other Irritants That Cause Allergies

Aside from food, we also have allergic reactions to other things: Airborne irritants such as pollen, contact allergies from shampoos and perfumes, pets, molds, household cleaning products, and even clothing can cause an allergic reaction. Remember, an allergic reaction is the body's immune system attempting to fight off something it perceives as an invader.

## Removing Allergic Foods Helps Behavior

More medical experts are now acknowledging that removing allergic foods from a child's diet can improve his behavior. James Braly, M.D., an allergy specialist, says that removing "provoking foods" from the diet can help reduce AD/HD in children. These "provoking foods" are the ones that the child "must have." When there is such a strong emotional connection to a particular food, it is probably one of the main culprits. Paul Marshall, Ph.D., from the University of Minnesota, is another expert who has found a strong relationship between food sensitivities and AD/HD. Dr. Marshall writes that children with AD/HD tend to have more food sensitivities than food allergies but that they can be allergic to other environmental toxins. Roger Katz, M.D., an allergy specialist from UCLA, has reported that 50 percent of his AD/HD referrals have true allergies.

## Dairy Allergies

Dairy is a major allergy culprit in children. In milk, it is the casein, a protein that is difficult to digest. A child who drinks milk and has more than five ear infections could be allergic to the casein in milk. If a child guzzles milk and hates cheese, this may indicate a casein allergy.

One of the leading experts in this field is Doris Rapp, M.D., a pediatrician who has written *Is This Your Child's World?* and *Is This Your Child?* She has found that dairy foods are a major allergen with children. Another pediatric specialist, Lendon Smith, M.D., has found that milk is a major problem for children. Dr. Smith correlates the relationship between upper respiratory infections and ear infections with the consumption of milk.

The truth is that we can get adequate calcium for our growth from vegetables. Calcium is not only important for good teeth and bones, it is vital for effective brain function.

## Wheat Allergies

Gluten, a protein found in wheat, is another common allergen in children. One of the problems is that wheat is found in almost everything we eat. Look at the labels of most pastas, cereals, and bread, and you will find wheat. And when we eat the same food continually, over time our bodies can become sensitized to it. Allergies also frequently occur with other foods, such as corn, peanuts, bacon (which contain nitrates and saturated fats), and syrup (which contains sugar and artificial flavorings).

## Hidden Allergies

In 1984, two researchers, Dwight Kalita, Ph.D., and William Philpott, M.D., found that certain hidden allergies affect brain function. With hidden allergies there are no overt symptoms or signals such as itching and sneezing, but these allergies can lead to physical and mental difficulties. In an article published in *Alternative Medical Review*, April 1998, Alan Gaby, M.D., from John Bastyr University in Seattle, Washington, wrote that avoiding foods that commonly cause allergies can help alleviate difficult-to-treat medical problems, including AD/HD.

The field of environmental medicine can help diagnose people who have these so-called hidden allergies and let them know what may be causing their problem. Some of these hidden allergies result from the consumption of heavy metals, pesticides, antibiotics, and growth hormones found in beef.

In her book, *Depression Cured at Last*, Sherry Rogers, M.D., a leading expert in environmental medicine, reported that brain allergies are hard to see because there are no overt signs and symptoms such as rashes or swelling. She says that some of the symptoms of brain allergies could be seizures, migraines, learning disorders, attention problems, violent mood swings, rage, autism, and panic attacks. These are also some of the signs and symptoms of AD/HD.

## Salicylates

Salicylates have been used for many hundreds of years to relieve pain. Aspirin is a form of synthesized acetyl salicylic acid, which has pain-relieving qualities. Salicylates work by passing through the blood-brain barrier to the brain to affect morphinelike substances, which reduce pain and increase our mood. However, for some children who are sensitive to salicylates, this product can affect the brain in a negative way. A child who is allergic to aspirin could also be allergic to naturally occurring salicylates in food. This sensitivity could be a contributing factor to AD/HD behavior. A simple urine test can determine if this sensitivity exists. Apples, apricots, cherries, grapes, peaches, plums, almonds, tomatoes, and raisins all contain naturally occurring salicylates. Peppermint, spearmint, and wintergreen also contain salicylates. You may find these mints in toothpaste, chewing gum, mouthwashes, and breath fresheners. Also, apple juice and grape juice are two common beverages children love to drink. They are also used as natural sweeteners, instead of sugar, in some products.

## Being the Detective

One of the best ways to determine which foods may be creating problems for yourself or your child is the elimination diet, where all suspicious foods are removed. There are many excellent resources for using an elimination diet, but here are the basics: It is important to sit with your child and other members of your family and explain what you are going to do. Everyone's cooperation is needed. Don't try to enact the diet when you are on vacation or at holiday time. Let the child's teacher know what you are doing and enlist her cooperation as well, because many children like to trade food during snack time.

Before starting the diet, keep a journal with a list of your child's symptoms, which you will be looking for later on. Identify the foods your child loves or craves. These are probably the biggest offenders. Particularly watch out for corn, eggs, chocolate, sugar, processed and packaged foods, peanuts, food colors and dyes, soft carbonated drinks, soy (tofu), chicken, beef, and wheat. Learn to read labels on everything. Sweeteners, such as modified cornstarch or dextrose, can be big offenders. Others, such as honey, sucrose, glucose corn sweetener, barley malt, and molasses, can be problems. Besides milk, other dairy products include lactose, whey, curd, yogurt, cheese, butter, and margarine.

In order for the elimination diet to be accurate, you must eliminate all suspicious foods completely. Even a tiny amount will ruin the accuracy of the test. If your child takes his own lunch to school, tell him that if he eats any food not on the diet to let you know because the diet must start all over at day one. Sometimes, telling the child this can be a good motivator.

After eliminating the suspicious foods, you may start to see your child's behaviors get worse for two or three days. This is just a withdrawal stage. In many instances, the food children eat gives them a lift. Without it, they may behave more irritably. This is an important juncture in the elimination diet because you may want to give them the food that is the offender. Don't!

If you can make it through to day four or five, your child's behavior should start to improve. On average, you will need to stay on the diet for five to ten days. Once the behavior has improved, you can challenge the child by giving him the suspected food to see if his behavior reverts back to that seen before the food was eliminated. If the good days do not occur, then your child probably has some other foods that need to be eliminated. Or there might be other hidden allergens, such as molds, dust, weeds, and trees. A physician who performs provocation/neutralization allergy testing can help pinpoint specific problems.

When success has been achieved through the elimination diet, begin the challenge procedure: Give one offending food to be eaten on an empty stomach. Symptoms can occur within a few minutes, or they may not occur for several hours or even until the next day. If a reaction does occur, do not give the food again. If the allergic reaction is severe, administer Alka Seltzer Gold, which will sometimes neutralize the reaction. The dosage is one tablet in water if a child is under twelve years of age, and two tablets in water for a child over twelve. If your child does not react to the food, it is safe for her to eat, and she may continue to do so.

The next day challenge with another food, unless the child's reaction from the previous day has not stopped. If that's the case, then wait until the reaction has stopped before giving another food.

When you have determined all the allergic foods to be avoided, start a rotation diet with foods that can be eaten. A rotation diet is the healthiest way to eat. Foods take about four days to be digested altogether. If you eat the same food while your body is still digesting it from previous consumption, then you are more likely to develop a sensitivity to that food. If you eat wheat on Monday, don't eat it again until Thursday.

If your child suffers from asthma or has swelling, be certain to seek the advice of your physician before embarking on the elimination diet.

## Oils and Fats

According to Michael A. Schmidt, M.D., in his groundbreaking book *Smart Fats*, vision, balance, reaction, and attention are directly related to brain function and neurological development. Dr. Schmidt says that the brain is about 60 percent fat.

How important are fats and oils to brain development? A group of doctors from Britain found that breast-fed children had IQs several points higher than those of children who were bottle-fed.[3] Breast milk contains fatty acids critical to brain development. Formula contains none of this fat.

## Link Between Omega-3 and Intelligence

In a study reported in the *American Journal of Clinical Nutrition*, fifty-three boys diagnosed with AD/HD had significantly lower concentrations of key fatty acids than did the control subjects.[4] Also, a subgroup of twenty-one subjects with AD/HD, who exhibited many symptoms of essential fatty acid deficiencies, had much lower levels of plasma concentrations than did thirty-two subjects with AD/HD but few essential fatty acid deficiency symptoms.[5]

Purdue University researchers found that people diagnosed with AD/HD had lower blood levels of the omega-3 fatty acid DHA (decosahexaenoic acid)—an important omega-3 fatty acid found in the brain and in higher concentrations in the retina.[6] Other researchers have found that academic performance, behavior, violence, and aggression were linked to dietary fats.

Scientists in *Nutrition Review* wrote in 1995 that children consume 30 percent more dietary fats than are needed. Many received over 10 percent from saturated fats, which is too much. The main sources were meat and dairy, which lack essential fatty acids. Children ate too much trans-fatty acids, in foods such as cookies, crackers, deserts, and candy. Not all fats are healthy and support a well-functioning nervous system and brain. Trans-fatty acids are harmful fats. These fats are derived from any oil heated for a long period of time, as in deep-frying. Trans-fatty acids are made from the hydrogenation process, used to manufacture margarine or shortening. Not only is there no nutritional value in trans-fatty acids, but they interfere with the function of the good fats, called unsaturated fats.

In one study reported by Dr. Schmidt, if a lactating mother has moderate to high levels of trans-fatty acids, her infant will receive those fatty acids from her breast milk. These trans-fatty acids interfere with the infant trying to synthesize the omega-3 fatty acids needed for brain and neurological development. To protect against trans-fatty acids in breast milk, a mother should restrict her dietary intake of them during conception, pregnancy, and lactation. Taking proper amounts of antioxidants will help protect the mother from unwanted toxins. And taking omega-3 fatty acids, or eating foods containing omega-3 fatty acids, will help develop a healthy brain and nervous system.

Avoid foods such as french fries, deep-fried fish burgers, corn chips, cookies, cake, mayonnaise, potato chips, puffed cheese snacks, candy, and partially hydrogenated soybean, sunflower, safflower, and corn oil.

Children diagnosed with AD/HD who have fatty acid imbalances can show the following symptoms: dry skin, increased thirst, frequent urination, dry hair, and allergies. Dr. E. A. Mitchell and colleagues, reporting their research in *Clinical Pediatrics* in 1987, discovered that children with AD/HD had low blood levels of DHA and arachidonic acid, two critically important brain-fats.[7] Dr. Mitchell's findings were supported by a Purdue University research study. Dr. Mitchell also found a higher ratio of omega-6 to omega-3 fatty acids. When this ratio gets too high, it may cause lower brain fats.

In 1996, a research group at Purdue found that ninety-six boys with lower levels of omega-3 fatty acids in their blood had more learning and behavioral problems than those whose omega-3 blood levels were normal.[8] Also, in 1996, L. J. Stevens reported in *Physiological Behavior* that an omega-3 deficiency was exhibited by behaviors of hyperactivity, impulsivity, anxiety, and temper tantrums.[9]

Sidney Baker, M.D., a former professor at Yale University School of Medicine and an expert in environmental medicine who has treated many children with AD/HD, found in another study that fatty acid balance is very important in treating a person with AD/HD. The key, according to Dr. Baker, is to look for skin changes.

## Fats and Brain Development

Seventy percent of the total brain, which will last our lifetime, has divided before birth. During gestation, the fetal brain may grow as many as 250,000 nerve cells each minute. At six weeks the growing brain makes up almost the entire embyro. During the next twelve weeks the brain is consuming about 70 percent of the energy delivered to the fetus. Proper fatty acid intake is critical during this period. The key is to supplement before conception. The developing brain needs DHA and arachidonic acid for proper growth and development, and there may be no opportunity to repair the damage from the effects of lack of omega-3 once the nervous system has formed. Therefore, the fetal brain, which develops quickly during pregnancy, needs DHA and arachidonic acid, and it can only be received from the mother. The baby robs the mother of these fatty acids by taking them from the placental blood, so the mother needs to resupply her body with them.

At birth, a baby's brain is comprised of 100 billion neurons. This is approximately the same amount of stars as are in the Milky Way. The infant's brain triples in size by the end of his first year. This rapid development is accomplished by the creation of synapses (nerve impulses communicating), the creation of branches, the covering of the nerves with myelin (a fatty substance), and the growth of existing nerve cells. The baby's brain develops the "hardwiring" for vision, movement, emotions, and language during the first year of life. This period becomes the formative time when the emotional, physical, and mental intelligence occurs. The neural pathways set the stage for development of speech, language, vision, gross and fine motor control, and emotional security. This process is the foundation for further development for years to come. Infancy is a critical period for formation of neuron connections that support the future years of learning.

During this first year, the brain requires almost 60 percent of the entire energy used by the infant. The majority of this energy is used to build the myelin sheath around the nerves and create the membranes of the nerve cells. High amounts of fatty acids are necessary since the infant's body cannot manufacture them effectively. If we compare an infant's fatty acid caloric intake with an adult's, the infant needs about 50 percent of its calories from fats as compared to the adult, who needs 20 to 30 percent of its calories from fats.

## Infant Development

Breast milk contains essential fatty acids necessary for brain development. Research reported in 1994 showed that breast-fed infants had higher IQs, better visual acuity, and higher protection against brain disorders in later life than did formula-fed babies, because they absorbed more essential fatty acids while nursing.[10]

An interesting cultural trend was studied in Inuit mothers from northern Quebec. The results indicated that although their diets were high in seal blubber, which contains a great deal of omega-3 fatty acids, the seals were found to be laced with organochlorine pesticides and PCBs. Inuit mothers displayed four to seven times higher levels of these toxins than non-Inuit mothers.[11] Although researchers expected to find more cases of AD/HD, developmental delays, and brain degeneration, this was not discovered. One 1994 report in *Science News* has suggested that omega-3 fatty acids partially protect against toxic chemicals.

## Vegetarians

Mothers who are vegetarians need to be concerned that they are not getting enough DHA, a deficiency that has been showing up in breast milk. Mothers with insufficient neural fatty acids in their own bodies provide less than what is needed to the developing fetus. Vegetarian mothers must be especially aware of the importance of having the proper fatty acids in their body to provide for the fetus's use. Vegetarians are usually deficient in DHA. It is critical for them to supplement. Because they don't eat fish, taking blue-green algae is one source, and taking flaxseed oil can increase the alpha-linolenic acid.

## Formula Versus Breast Milk

Before 1998, formula-fed infants did not receive DHA in their milk because it was not added to formula until that time. In some studies, formula-fed babies have not performed as well as breast-fed babies on visual, attention, and intelligence tests. If proper fatty acid balance can be achieved at a very young age, less chance exists for learning, behavioral, or other brain-related problems. In a study conducted at Purdue University, breast-fed children showed less AD/HD behavior. The longer the period for breast-feeding, the less likelihood for AD/HD. Breast milk has more fatty acids for brain development.

Another important factor is that there needs to be the proper balance between omega-3 and omega-6 fatty acids during pregnancy. The developing fetus needs more omega-3 fatty acids, and if they are not received, there can be a higher incidence of learning, behavioral, or visual problems.

Essential fatty acid deficiency also may result during pregnancy because of physiologic stress. Pregnant women should take fatty acid supplements if adequate amounts are not supplied by their diets. Sources of omega-3 fatty acids include flaxseed, pumpkin seed, canola, and walnut oils. The following oils need to be balanced by omega-3: borage, evening primrose, sesame, and black currant seed.

Dr. Ralph Holman of the University of Minnesota found in his research that women should consume more DHA fats because the fetal nervous system needs these fats during pregnancy.[12] However, it does not stop here. During childbearing years, it is important for the mothers to monitor their amount of dietary fat balance. According to Dr. Monique Al's research, a mother's DHA stores were depleted more and more with each pregnancy. DHA is found in coldwater fish (eat organic when possible): salmon, mackerel, herring, sardines, trout, albacore tuna, and caviar. (These are also good sources of omega-3.)

Chicken eggs contain DHA if the chicken is fed high omega-3 fatty acid.[13]

Taking 1 to 2 teaspoons of primrose oil or flaxseed oil per day will supply the body with enough essential fatty acids. If this oil is bitter tasting, then it is spoiled and should not be taken. Other sources include nuts, avocados, olive oil, and organic canola oil.

Any food with shortening in it increases shelf life but decreases the function of the brain. Bad fats deplete good fats. Symptoms of a deficiency in essential fatty acids include dry skin, wax in ears, toe walking, tight muscles, excessive drinking of water, and flaky skin like eczema.

## Other Important Factors About Fats and Oils

Buy organic oils. Also, try to get your oils from food sources such as fish, walnuts, flaxseed, and sesame seeds. Flaxseeds contain lignans, which have health benefits, and chemicals are not applied to them during the growing process. Oils should be stored in dark bottles and kept covered because exposure to light and air can increase rancidity. Warm temperatures can also spoil oils; keep them refrigerated. Ghee and coconut oils don't need to be refrigerated. Oils should be unrefined so that there is more of the original product available. Oils should be cold-processed and expeller pressed—this will be indicated on the label. Oil that tastes bitter is probably rancid.

Cooking destroys and damages oils. Cook with fats such as butter, ghee, olive oil, or coconut oil. One way to avoid damaging good tasting oils is to sauté foods with water in a pan or skillet until just below boiling. As food is cooked, add a small amount of oil. This will decrease the heat contact with the oil and preserve the flavor. Don't heat oils to the smoking point.

Although butter contains no omega-3 fatty acids, it is better than margarine, which contains trans-fatty (bad) acids. When using butter, it is best that it be organic to avoid antibiotics and growth hormones. Ghee is a good substitute for butter. It is used in Ayurvedic medicine to support physical and mental renewal. It is a great cooking oil and does not oxidize even at high temperatures. Although ghee does not contain essential fatty acids needed for the brain, it has great healing properties for the body.

To summarize, balance the amount of essential fatty acids in the body according to the individual. Include in your diet fatty acids that are necessary for brain function and brain development. Remember, fat intake should be only 20 to 30 percent of your total diet. Saturated fats should be limited. Omega-3 to omega-6 ratio in the blood should be between 1:1 and 3:1. (Blood tests can determine fatty acid levels.)

Vitamins $B_6$, $B_3$, magnesium, and vitamin C help the body utilize fatty acids. Omega-3 unsaturated fats should not be used for cooking. Avoid trans-fatty acids, and supplement with antioxidants, which help to protect brain membranes.

Remember these three crucial points:

1. Essential fat is fat that is absolutely necessary for the regulation of every bodily function.
2. Essential fat is fat that must be included because it cannot be made in the body.
3. Essential fat is fat that has not been altered from its natural state by faulty cooking, food processing, pesticides, and herbicides.

# CHAPTER 8

# Developmental Milestones, Learning, and Fun

W hat is learning? Learning is the ability to acquire knowledge or understanding. Conditions requiring some problem solving are necessary for learning to take place. Learning can involve using one's body, one's mind, or both together. This requires some degree of self-awareness and flexibility so that if the person has difficulty attempting to solve the problem one way, she can learn from what she has tried and apply it to the next attempt to solve the problem. It helps if the environment is supportive, which means that guidance can be given, if necessary, to help the person self-discover the answer. Criticism or negativity only hurts the development of learning skills.

Training that creates a conditioned response is not learning. The key in learning is to arrange the conditions so that the person can make the discovery on her own by letting it happen, not by forcing it or straining. Sometimes in order for learning to occur, a person needs to change her belief system about how to approach a certain problem. This requires a change in one's attitude.

In an article entitled "Getting Out of the Way," Naomi Aldort makes some excellent points about working with children.[1] She gives the example of watching her two-year-old immerse himself while playing the piano. One day he amazingly played a smooth scale, and that night, when his father came home, Naomi excitedly asked her son to play the scale again. He refused to do this "trick" and did not play that scale for many weeks afterward. Only when it was in his self-interest did he attempt it again. The article points out that praising a child's every activity leads to conditioning, while a parent's self-discipline to observe encourages the child's personal curiosity. Praising drives the child to succeed, while personal curiosity allows the child to delight in what he learns.

Children need to follow their own drummers by free choice and self-learning. Otherwise, we are creating a child whose self-esteem is dependent on performing or meeting the expectations of his parents. Almost every child has the skill to open like a flower to full blossom. Children who are given the opportunity to develop their own skills and knowledge will grow and prosper.

The labels placed on children because they can't function as expected in a classroom are at best a poor method of trying to deal with their learning challenges. Children are unique in their expression. If a child does not fit into a certain mold, then labels serve only to classify and place limitations on him. Instead, there are other options available.

This chapter discusses the importance of the sensory-motor system and what activities can be done to stimulate learning and development.

## Learning Is Dependent on Motor and Cognitive Development

Arnold Gesell, M.D., said that the cycles of development are interdependent and that all childhood development proceeds in a systematic, sequential manner.[2]

Jean Piaget, Swiss psychologist and child development expert, said that motor experiences are the foundation for mental development and that children progress through their development in various stages.[3]

Thinking is based on motor activity. In early life, motor activity develops before thinking, then they work together, and finally thinking precedes the child's movement. However, in the developmental sequence, motor activity is critical for learning on a cognitive level. For example, in order for visual tracking and hand-eye coordination to be working well for reading, the general motor development must be solid and automatic in its function. General motor activities include walking, standing, and balancing. Development goes from general motor skills to fine motor skills. Large muscles move small muscle groups. Children with developmental delays and learning disabilities usually have difficulty with balance and coordination. Instead, they would rather watch TV or play on the computer to avoid movement activities. Working with the whole brain trains the whole body.

Dr. Gerald Getman, a behavioral/developmental optometrist who has made great contributions to the field of child development and learning, also found that learning and development take place in a specific sequence. First, the child learns to move his arms, hands, legs, and feet so he can explore his environment. Obviously, his eyes are the steering mechanism for the body. Dr. Getman called this general motor development. Second, the child learns to use the eyes and hands to manipulate his world, which is called specific motor development. Third, the child learns efficient visual tracking (eye movement) patterns to understand his world without having to move or explore. Dr. Getman called this phase of moving the eyes without having to move the body to learn phase 3: oculomotor development. Fourth, the child uses vision and movement experiences to communicate with others. This helps the child establish a relationship between vision and language that supports the exchange of information through speech. Fifth, the child learns visualization skills, which help interpret and perceive similarities and differences between numbers and words. This helps him understand symbols and language.

## Children's Developmental Milestones

Listed below are a child's developmental milestones. If a child does not reach these milestones in the course of her natural development, it could indicate a problem later on. Still, every child is individual and may not be exactly on schedule, so it is important not to push your child to reach these milestones. Allow your child to self-discover so that her learning and development proceed in the order and sequence that are natural for her to be fully integrated into her sensory-motor skills.[4]

### Sensory-Motor Skills

- Sits alone at eight months
- Crawls alone at nine months
- Stands alone at fifteen months
- Walks alone at fifteen months

### Teething

- Two lower central incisors at six to nine months
- Four upper incisors at eight to twelve months
- One lower lateral incisor at twelve to fifteen months
- Four canines at eighteen to twenty-four months
- Four posterior molars at twenty-four to thirty months

### Elimination

- Bowel control at twelve to twenty-four months
- Bladder control at two to three years

## Dressing

- Buttons clothes at four years
- Laces shoes at five years

## Speech

- Syllables at six months
- "Da-da" at nine months
- Two words at twelve months
- Four words at fifteen months
- Short sentences at twenty-four months
- Gives full name at thirty months

Listed below are activities that can be done to stimulate normal developmental milestones. They are broken down by age.[5]

## Activities: One to Three Months

- Talk to the baby wherever you are together in a room.
- If the baby does not move around in her crib, then move her position within the crib and move the crib to different positions, so that both sides of her peripheral vision can be stimulated.
- Encourage the baby to develop and repeat patterns.
- Casting a shadow behind a mobile can be interesting to her.
- Change the baby's position while she's feeding to allow her to change her focus.

## Activities: Four to Eight Months

- If the baby is lying on his stomach, let him try to get up on his own. It is important that he lift his head and develop strong neck muscles. Let him spend time on his stomach.

- Create a mobile that the child can touch with his hands, so he can explore moving objects with both his eyes and hands at the same time.
- Encourage him to use his feet as well.
- Show the baby different objects of different sizes, weights, colors, and textures.
- Set up an obstacle course to encourage crawling in and around objects.
- Verbally label objects as he plays with them and ask him to find an object by calling it by its name.
- Let the infant be on the floor as much as possible.
- Don't pick her up when she is crying.
- Massage her hands and feet as much as possible.
- Don't sit her up until she is seven months old.

## Activities: Nine to Eighteen Months

- Have the child play side by side with another child her own age.
- Continue to use an obstacle course for crawling, walking, and pushing/pulling toys.
- Under close supervision, provide the child with small objects, such as beads or buttons, to handle and play with.
- Provide fat crayons and paper to scribble on.
- Allow her to draw and write on a chalkboard.
- Encourage the child to stack blocks, pillows, and objects.

## Activities: Eighteen Months to Three Years

- Play baseball (catch and pitch) with a balloon.
- Read books together, and have him point to the pictures and describe differences between the pictures.
- Provide a large set of blocks or Legos.
- Encourage climbing, swinging, sliding, twisting, and turning.

- Play games that involve kicking and running using a beach ball.
- Set up a safe situation for the child to cut out pictures using scissors.
- Provide clay or Play-Doh.

### Activities: Three to Four Years

- Play matching games using pictures that are very different.
- Encourage rolling, tumbling, and balancing activities.
- Do a daily read-out-loud session, and have the child point to each picture while you are reading.
- Allow the child to act out a story you have read to him, giving him free expression.
- Introduce the child to rollerblading and bicycle riding.

### Activities: Four to Five Years

- Have her take care of a pet.
- Encourage board and card games.
- Encourage roller blading, bike riding, skipping, and skiing. The movement should be a visually guided movement. Have the child go to the right, then left, in a circle, and through an obstacle course.
- Encourage the child to describe things in a room. Guide her descriptions with leading questions that encourage her to relate things to one another, but do not tell her what to look for or answer the questions for her. Allow her to tell you what she discovers.

## Five Levels of Brain Processing

In helping a child develop, there are five levels of brain processing: visual-motor, speech/language/auditory, kinesthesia/tactile/proprioception, vestibular, and motor. I would classify motor skills as both gross motor skills and fine motor skills. Gross motor skills involve big muscle coordination like skipping, running, balancing, and bike riding. Specific motor development involves ocular motor (eye movements), fingers, throat, and tongue.

The different levels of brain processing can be encouraged with the following suggestions:[6]

## Kinesthesia/Tactile/Proprioception (Capable of Receiving Stimuli Originating in Muscles, Tendons, and Other Internal Tissues)

Provide as much stimulation as possible. Plastic letters and numbers can be felt with eyes closed to connect touch with visualization. Hide a variety of objects in a bag and have the child identify what he is feeling. Practice writing words and numbers in sand or clay. Practice finger painting.

Provide for lots of crashing into pillows. Allow the child to push and pull and carry as many things as possible. Use wheelbarrow walking, walking and running through obstacle courses, and horseback riding as ways to stimulate proprioception. Swimming is also a way to provide deep touch and proprioception.

## Vestibular

Encourage the child to roll on the ground, swing, run, hang upside down, and spin. Play tetherball or balloon volleyball. Have the child roll and bounce up and down on a physioball on both her tummy and back.

## Speech/Language/Auditory

Encourage the child to identify sounds and nature noises. Can she organize the sounds into different categories? Listen to music using the Mozart effect (described in chapter 9).

## Visual-Motor Development

Use colors to stimulate vision. Encourage all forms of artwork. Play song games like head, shoulders, knees, and toes. Play patty cake. Play twister, hide and seek, dot to dot, and visual maze games.

## Motor Coordination

After diet is improved, work on increasing muscle tone, strength, endurance, and postural control. Swing, climb, and hang from monkey bars; and push and pull heavy objects. Play hopscotch, one-legged races, and balance-beam games. Encourage belly crawling, which will help the interweaving of upper and lower extremities, lateral trunk flexibility, motor planning, and antigravity postural responses.

Encourage riding a bike, roller blading, skiing, or skating. All these activities should be done slowly with a visually guided movement to improve fine motor control.

Some other general activities, which should be done in this order, include:

- Balancing on each foot with eyes open and closed
- Hopping
- Crosspattern crawling, walking, running while swinging arms and legs in a cross-patterning movement
- Skipping
- Jump rope
- Swimming
- Martial arts
- Gymnastics

## Activities for Daily Living

It is important to incorporate into a child's daily routine activities that will encourage learning and development. We don't want to just train conditioned responses; we want children to grow and learn to think for themselves.

Children can select their own clothing and get themselves ready for the day. They can also independently brush their own hair and teeth. To develop math skills, ask them to measure recipe ingredients. Stirring the ingredients together helps to develop upper extremity strength and coordination. Sequencing is encouraged by asking what the child did yesterday and what is scheduled for him to do today.

These steps should be included, and they are as important as any activity that is done with your child:[7]

- Honor your child's existence.
- Give her choices; don't be a dictator.
- Never belittle him.
- Make her partners in her own upbringing.
- Explain to an infant what you are doing even though he may not understand you. This sets up the consciousness for him to communicate with you when he gets older.
- Test your child before giving her medicine.
- Don't criticize him.
- Guide your child, but let her decide what and who she wants to be.
- Know that he may get tired easily and not be able to focus, that he needs extra time and more awareness, and that he cannot burn the candle at both ends.
- Be a partner in setting limits for her.
- Listen to him and respect him in all ways.
- Don't ever try to deceive her.
- Don't abuse him.
- Don't lie to her.

Children are very special people. Honor their uniqueness.

## Behavioral Optometry?

Any sensory-motor learning programs need to be presented and taught in a specific order because learning and development naturally occur in a certain sequence. When you build a house you have to build the foundation first before putting in the plumbing, then insulation before the roofing. Learning how to learn is more effective if the skills are taught in the proper order. Otherwise, what you are doing is teaching the child to be effective at specific activities, but the child is not able to fully integrate his sensory-motor skills. Remember, shotgun approaches don't work.

## ∾ Adrian

Adrian is a beautiful eight-year-old girl who was adopted from an orphanage in India at age six months. Her mother brought Adrian in for evaluation because she was having difficulty reading, learning, and concentrating. We found no significant nutritional or developmental learning problems per se, but the first six months of her life were anything but normal. It is sometimes difficult to ascertain the developmental history of adopted children; however, most of them are at a higher risk for developing learning and behavioral problems. My evaluation found some motor development skills, such as balance, right-left organization, and fine motor development, to be about two years below Adrian's chronological age. In addition to a homeopathic protocol, a developmental-learning motor program was recommended.

## What Is a Developmental-Learning Program?

Dr. Albert A. Sutton, a leader in developmental optometry, has been designing developmental-learning programs for many years. According to Dr. Sutton, a developmental-learning program is a series of activities designed to help a child or adult learn sensory-motor and cognitive skills on an automatic, subconscious level. The intention of the program is to help the foundation skills of attention, focus, flexibility, and detail focusing, which are basic to learning. When these skills become automatic, a person is better able to perform more advanced tasks successfully.[8]

In addition to the child being taken through the developmental-learning activities by a trained professional, the program is usually taught to the parents so that they can carry it out every day at home. The regularity and consistency of the daily activities make the program effective. The activities are planned in a sequential order so that learning can take place in the proper order. This order assures that the child learns and develops his skills effectively and deeply.

The child is required to spend at least thirty minutes a day, five days per week on this sensory-motor program. Sometimes it is necessary to break down each daily session into two or three shorter periods. The key is the intensity and regularity of each daily session. Some activities may require more or less time, however each activity should be done until progress is adequate, before moving to the next activity in the sequence.

Each session of the learning program starts with warm-up exercises. These warm-ups should be continued daily even after progress is seen through the developmental-learning activities. Two of my other favorite warm-ups are "long swings" and "deep breathing."

Long swings should be done by the child in bare feet for about five minutes per day. Standing upright and balanced on both feet, the child swings her upper body first to one side, then to the other, while keeping her feet stationary. During the swing she is not looking at anything in particular, just scanning the horizon and watching the world go by; but as the swing reaches its farthest point on either side, the child should look over her shoulder and fix her eyes on a target (as the anchor for stabilizing orientation). This activity helps her develop the peripheral vision ambient system more effectively.

Deep breathing also should be done in bare feet for about five minutes per day. The child moves his arms, eyes, and body up with full nasal inhales and down on full mouth exhales in continuous rhythmic movements. During this breathing practice, make sure the child is breathing into his stomach. Shallow breathing into the lungs and chest does not help the relaxation process.

These warm-up exercises awaken the child's mind and are used before every developmental-learning session.

As the child's performance improves, more activities are added. It is important to keep raising the level of difficulty so that the child has to stretch her ability. Goal setting is an essential ingredient of any program because it helps the child see progress on a daily basis, which makes her feel successful. These goals need to be discussed with the child, and the child should meet or beat her goals from the previous day.

When doing this program, after the directions are given, the activities are done in free style, without a critique from the parents. The child begins to get the feel of it with sequence, continuity, rhythm, and flow. It is important not to interrupt the child's rhythm and flow to correct errors, because it is very important for the child to self-discover. When there is any discrepancy between the directions given and the performance of the child, a method called Socratic Guidance is used to help the child see his discrepancy.

## The Socratic Method

Children do not get bored or lose concentration if they are actively participating when using the Socratic method, when they are guided and led by someone who questions their thinking. Sometimes it is important to challenge the child's answers and ask him if he can defend a certain position.

This method takes some energy when you are moving a child in a certain direction. You should ask very specific questions, which are as logically leading as possible. That is part of the point of the method. Not just any question will do, particularly not broad, open-ended questions like "What is balancing?" Instead, you might ask, "How did you balance for one minute without falling over?"

It is important that parents understand their child's developmental level and what prior knowledge their child may have that will help her assimilate what you want her to learn. This encourages the child to think and understand, rather than teaching her to give a conditioned response or an interpretation of what she thinks you want her to say.

These are the three important points about the questions:

1. They must be interesting or intriguing to the child.
2. They must lead the child by incremental and logical steps (from the child's prior knowledge or understanding) in order that he can readily answer. At some point, the questions must head toward a conclusion, not just individual, isolated points.
3. They must be designed to get the child to see particular points. We are essentially trying to get children to think on their own by using their own logic. In that way they can see by their own reflections on your questions, either the good new ideas or the obviously erroneous ideas that are the consequences of their established ideas, knowledge, or beliefs. You cannot ask just any question or just start anywhere.

Finally, two of the interesting, perhaps side benefits of using the Socratic method are that it gives children a chance to experience the joy and excitement of discovering (often complex) ideas on their own. And it gives parents a chance to learn how much more inventive and bright children are than they usually appear to be when they are primarily passive.

# CHAPTER 9

# Complementary Treatments That Work!

There are many causes for AD/HD. But I have found that there are no hard-and-fast rules when treating this condition; because of its complexity, it requires a multidisciplinary approach. Many complementary treatments offered in the marketplace have been proven to be safe and effective alternatives to the use of drugs. But usually there's no single magic bullet. Parents need to understand that four different modalities may be needed, with a 25 percent benefit from each approach to reach the desired result. The approach to treat each child will be as individual as the child. Sometimes one or the other of these modalities is introduced at different phases of treatment. And these effective treatments must be incorporated into an overall plan in different combinations.

Usually my extensive history form and checklist guide me toward the best avenue to take in each case. I also may begin a certain treatment protocol and observe how the parents and child are responding, then alter treatment based on their responses. Finally, in most cases, these treatments take a great deal longer than traditional medications. But seeing your child, unaltered by drugs, become healthy and balanced, able to adjust and learn, is worth it in the end.

Three treatment approaches, in particular, are highly effective in naturally reducing symptoms of AD/HD and helping the person reconnect to his own healing mechanisms:

- Treatments that address processing of sensory information, including sensory-motor integration, vision therapy, syntonic light therapy, and auditory training
- Treatments to boost the immune system, including homeopathic cell salts and essential oils
- Structural therapies, including osteopathy, cranial-sacral therapy, and chiropractic

First, the child must be evaluated holistically by a health practitioner. This is accomplished through a detailed history, which helps to determine what influences from the past are affecting the child today. One must start by looking all the way back to the in utero period. Next, the child's nutritional and biochemical levels need to be thoroughly investigated.

As discussed in chapter 4, the primitive survival reflexes need to be evaluated by a trained professional. If these reflexes are not inhibited, a motor development program needs to be instituted to help inhibit the reflexes. After that program is in place, then several gross motor, fine motor, and cognitive skills should be developed. To determine what areas need to be addressed, testing needs to be done in the motor development, vision, and speech-language/auditory areas.

However, it is very important that the child not be compartmentalized by a health practitioner who is not able to look at the whole picture. Remember, we are a series of interrelated parts. Any sensory-motor program needs to involve all aspects of the child. If the speech/language therapist does not work with the occupational therapist or vision therapist, then the child may improve individual skills in one category but be unable to integrate all the therapies together because they are presented in a segmented fashion. Since all these sensory-motor systems originate in the brain, we are really assessing the child's brain development.

## A Holistic Approach to Vision Development

Acuity, or 20/20 vision, is only one aspect of vision development. An analysis by behavioral/developmental optometrists goes beyond optical correction or eye health. Our specialty considers a child's vision in relationship to the other neurological and sensory systems of the body.

In my experience, vision problems can be secondary to immune issues, metabolic disorders, dietary considerations, or other sensory-processing problems. Once these factors are addressed, in many cases modalities such as vision therapy are even more effective because the child has an increased capacity for learning and development.

## More Vision Problems Today

### ❀ Richard

Richard was a ten-year-old who suffered from headaches in the afternoon. His performance in school had slipped. He was no longer in the highest reading group, and his grades went from Bs to Cs in spelling and math. My evaluation showed that Richard's eye focus broke apart when he attempted to move both eyes at the same time. He also focused much more with his right eye than with his left. Much of Richard's headaches and tension problem was the result of his efforts to see the print in his books.

Instead of Richard being free to use his energy for creativity and higher degrees of problem solving, he had to focus his attention on trying to keep the print clear enough to read. This continuous stress interfered with his learning process.

## ⚮ Tim

Tim was a fourth-grader who read on a second-grade level. He confused his right from his left and reversed his Bs and Ds. He could not concentrate for more than five minutes at a time, and the frustration he and his parents experienced was very painful. Tim had been tested by the school and labeled as learning disabled.

During his vision evaluation, I discovered that Tim could only follow a moving target with his eyes by moving his whole head. When he tried to move only his eyes, the quality of the movement was erratic and jerky. He also could not use both sides of his body together, only one side at a time. Being able to tell Tim that he had a specific vision imbalance that was interfering with his learning and that he could do something to eliminate the problem provided much relief to him and his parents.

After two months of vision therapy, Tim brought his reading up to grade level, his other grades improved to Bs and As, and he began to play baseball. His dyslexia pattern was significantly reduced.

It is important to know that not all dyslexia patterns are reduced as quickly as in Tim's case. However, if you or your child have learning difficulties or have been labeled with dyslexia or ADD, at least have a vision system evaluation by a behavioral optometrist. Every bit helps!

## Learning Disabilities Equal Illiteracy

There seems to be a higher incidence of learning disabilities and child illiteracy over the past fifteen years. In the United States, when a child falls two years or more behind in reading and writing, he or she is legally classified as learning disabled. Dr. Alan Cott says that there are about ten million children who suffer from some type of learning disability. Yet, there is still the push in most schools (and by many parents) for children to read earlier, to get better grades, to succeed, to produce greater results, and to perform.

What are some probable reasons for these perceived difficulties? Perhaps children actually learn differently than the way they are taught. Perhaps a child's visual system is not ready to begin reading at age six. Instead of teaching reading at this age, suppose we allow intuitive, creative expression, and offer more movement in the classroom. Perhaps we need to reduce the importance of grades, of excelling, or being product-oriented until a child reaches age twelve. Perhaps the true art of teaching is watching how each child can absorb and learn.

Two other areas needing our particular attention are special education classes and dyslexia. In the special education classes we need to have more comprehensive visual screening and to incorporate some visual activities into the curriculum in order to improve the visual-processing abilities of the children. There are many children in these classes who can see the 20/20 distance acuity chart but have difficulties with skills such as tracking, focusing, and visual coordination. Many of these vision imbalances go undetected, and the special education classrooms become nothing more than dumping grounds filled with children who aren't learning disabled at all but have a learning style that doesn't conform to the school's methods of teaching. Incorporating visual-motor activities involving visual tracking, eye-body coordination, visual memory, and spatial relationship puzzles to stimulate vision, movement, intuition, and creativity would go a long way to make learning and reading more productive and positive experiences.

## Dyslexia

Dyslexia describes a specific reading disability. It is a coding problem. A person has difficulty breaking the code of language. Dyslexia occurs when the brain has difficulty interpreting the symbols of written language. The key is early diagnosis, multidisciplinary care, counseling, and the appropriate educational intervention and remediation. Behavioral optometrists who work with visually related learning and reading problems can serve a key role in the co-management of patients with learning or attention problems.

In an exciting 1986 study using a computerized testing process, Dr. George Pavlidis proved that "dyslexic" preschoolers exhibited irregular eye movements.[1] Since vision therapy works with the sensory, motor, and neuromuscular systems—improving the visual tracking and visual sequencing skills—it can be an effective tool for working with children labeled dyslexic.

Vision therapy is not a substitute for education. The purpose of vision therapy is to remove the interference so that tutoring, remedial education, counseling, and occupational therapy can be more effective and lasting. The tragedy is that teachers and parents are not educated about visual problems. If a child can be diagnosed in kindergarten before he experiences the negative feelings, conflict, and failure, much of the struggle can be avoided.

The vision difficulties children experience are caused by many factors. Vision is a learned skill. A child learns to use vision by interacting with the environment through movement. That is why creeping and crawling are very important milestones in a child's development. If there is a childhood trauma or sickness, a lag in development can occur in the visual, auditory, vestibular, kinesthetic, or motor systems. Sometimes if the in utero or birthing experience is not normal, there can be a lag in development of any of the information-gathering systems, including vision.

On average, a child's vision system does not fully develop until age twelve. An overload with schoolwork in primary grades can stress the vision system and cause a breakdown in the visual skills of the child.

Our society is a long way from agreement on this question, but we can ask, "How much do attitude and self-esteem affect learning?" My experience is that they are very important. Children need a lot of love, support, nurturing, and positive experiences to feel as though they belong in the world.

It is important for teachers, resource-room specialists, psychologists, guidance counselors, school nurses, and physicians to make a connection between observable behaviors and vision problems.

These are some of the physical symptoms to look for:

- Red, sore, or tired eyes
- Excessive blinking, eye rubbing, or squinting
- Closing an eye or tilting the head when reading
- Complaints of blurred or double vision
- An eye turning in or out; erratic and jerky eye movements
- Sensitivity to sunlight or fluorescent lighting

One of the reasons children are experiencing more vision-related problems is the amount of television they watch every day. The average fourth-grader watches too many hours of television on a daily basis. First, watching television is a very passive experience. It programs us to sit in a trancelike state, discouraging any kind of creative problem solving. Children need a variety of general and specific motor experiences to develop their brains and bodies fully. Stimulating vision development requires movement, creative thinking, and self-awareness. One way to encourage healthy vision development is to limit the amount of television watched.

The increased use of computers and computer games also contributes to poor visual skills. Using your eyes on a computer requires the eye muscles to focus in one position for a long period of time. If the visual skills are not fully developed, then the visual system cannot handle the stress, and this can cause problems. Again, proper vision development requires movement using the eyes, brain, and body. Sitting at a computer for long periods of time does not nurture and support a healthy visual system.

## Developmental Optometry's Long Lineage

A child who is underachieving and having difficulty with focus and concentration rarely has an eye problem but may have a vision problem. For over fifty years optometrists have worked with children with healthy eyes who see clearly (20/20) at a distance and near but have vision problems. One needs to look at the development of vision and the development of the whole child to really understand the child's capability for learning. Movement is key for learning to take place. For learning to occur in the brain, it must first start in the muscles of the body.

In 1928, Dr. A. M. Skeffington started the Optometric Extension Program, an organization responsible for teaching vision therapy to optometrists. He made many contributions to the field of optometry and introduced many concepts. First, he said that vision is a mode of information processing with a feedback loop. He also said that sensory and motor integration is the basis and foundation for learning; that central-peripheral vision is important for efficient vision; and that vision and learning are interrelated. He treated the patient as a total integrated human being, and he brought together many different professionals from various disciplines. One of his greatest contributions (and he had many) was creating a climate for introducing new ideas, which he synthesized from all these other professionals. He was a visionary.

Listed below are the tenets of developmental vision care developed by Dr. Skeffington:[2]

- Vision is dominant, a component of one's actions; it monitors and controls nearly all actions.
- Vision is information processing.
- Vision is motor, output, guiding, directing, monitoring, and movement.
- Vision is learned and developed.
- Vision is affected by posture.
- Physical adaptations can occur due to internal and external stress from the environment.
- Adverse adaptations can cause vision problems that reduce visual efficiency.
- Vision problems can develop into eye problems.
- Vision problems are reversible, hence visual problems are preventable.

## Other Developmental Optometrists

In our field of behavioral/developmental optometry, there is a group of doctors who embrace and practice with a holistic philosophy. One doctor who has led the profession with his research and clinical practice is Dr. Albert A. Sutton, who runs the Center for Learning in Tamarac, Florida. A leader in developmental optometry who practices with a holistic approach, Dr. Sutton was one of the developmental optometrists who worked alongside Dr. Arnold Gesell in his research lab at the Gesell Institute studying infant and child development. He has taught on the graduate level in the field of education for seventeen years at Barry University in Miami and has been involved in research with neuroscientists and physicians concerning the brain, vision, and nutrition.

Conducting a study of the effects of nutrition on learning, Dr. Sutton teamed up with Dr. Alan Cott and the Miami Heart Institute, where two groups of children received developmental-vision-learning programs. Group A received an additional nutritional assessment and dietary recommendations, while Group B did not. Group A scored much higher on the posttesting than did Group B. The study was repeated so that Group B then received nutritional support while Group A did not. Both groups still received the developmental-vision-learning program. But this time Group B scored better on the testing. The results showed a child's biochemistry and nutrition on his learning and development.[3]

One of the significant tests Dr. Sutton invented is the Mind-Body Evaluation, a battery of tests utilizing the importance of vision, movement, rhythm and timing, and dominance. It is a very effective way to evaluate how a child learns and moves—two prerequisites for proper development.

Dr. Sutton has also been designing developmental-learning programs for many years. The programs, he says, are a series of activities that help a child or adult learn sensory-motor and cognitive skills on an automatic, subconscious level. The intention of the programs is to help provide the foundation skills of attention, focus, flexibility, and detail focusing, which are so basic to learning. When these skills become automatic, a person is better able to perform more advanced tasks successfully. In addition to the child being taken through the developmental-learning activities by a trained professional, the program is usually taught to the parents so that they can carry it out every day at home.

Dr. John Streff and Dr. Richard Apell were developmental optometrists who worked at the Visual Research Department of the Gesell Institute in Connecticut during the early 1960s. One of the many aspects of developmental optometry, which they researched, was the use of developmental low plus lenses and the effects the lenses have on a child's visual performance. According to Drs. Apell and Streff, these lenses, if prescribed accurately, could help a child learn to center and focus the eyes and brain in more effective ways. In some cases, this could make a profound impact on the child's ability to read.

Dr. Elliot Forrest, also a developmental optometrist, was a leader in the field. One of his many contributions was a book entitled *Stress and Vision*, which discusses how our mental states, beliefs, attitudes, and biases are highly influential in creating what we see and how we use our vision. Dr. Albert Shankman took Dr. Forrest's work even further in his book, *Vision Enhancement Training*, which describes concentration as putting the mind and eyes on the same object at the same time effortlessly. His descriptions and exercises combine some of the yoga and Ayurvedic philosophies and are a holistic approach to teaching more effective visual concentration and attention.

Dr. Kenneth C. Koslowe, O.D., M.S., performed an interesting study linking binocular vision problems (both eyes are not working together, and depth perception is not normal) to some learning disabilities.[4] He performed a study at a multidisciplinary clinic that treated students with various learning problems. Dr. Koslowe found that 41 out of 100 children tested were diagnosed with a binocular vision difficulty that could be remedied through the use of developmental lenses and vision therapy.

In another study, Dr. Martin H. Birnbaum found that in managing children with reading and learning problems it is crucial to assess a child's vision as one factor that could interfere with a child's ability to read and learn. He found that vision not only plays a role in reading, but also in other aspects of the classroom performance.[5] For example, written arithmetic requires accurate eye movements, perceptual and spatial skills to accurately copy from the board, or to copy neatly spaced or aligned columns of numbers on a page. He also reported that children need visualization and conceptual relationship skills in order to do higher forms of arithmetic.

Dr. Birnbaum found that spelling requires visual imagery and visualization skills, especially if a child is a good reader and phonetic coding skills are adequate, and yet the child struggles with his spelling.

## Visual Information Processing and Reading Difficulties

An area of research that has been getting a lot of attention is the parallel association between visual information processing and reading difficulties. A study conducted by Gary Sigler and Todd Wylie tested the efficacy of vision therapy as it related to IQ and achievement. Specifically, the researchers surveyed seventy-three learning-disabled readers, of which thirty-seven were found to have visual focusing and visual coordination problems. Of the thirty-seven subjects treated, the results showed that reading performance improved in both reading rate and comprehension.[6]

## Scotopic Sensitivity Syndrome

Helen Irlen has proposed a condition she calls scotopic sensitivity syndrome. She claims that many people diagnosed dyslexic have scotopic sensitivity and that the treatment of choice is specially tinted lenses. Mitchell Scheiman studied the relationship between visual problems and the Irlen filter candidates and found that 95 percent of those tested actually had undetected vision problems.[7] W. C. Maples and Lut Helsen conducted a study to determine if actual visual problems existed in adults who had been unsuccessful in school. Using the same testing criteria as the Scheiman study, the results showed that 100 percent of the subjects tested had significant visual problems.[8] Therefore, any person with a learning or reading problem should, at the very least, have a developmental vision evaluation to rule out undetected vision problems.

Stanley Kaseno, a behavioral optometrist from California, has proven that there is a strong correlation between undiagnosed vision problems, academic nonachievement, and juvenile delinquency.[9]

Clearly, not all learning difficulties are vision related. Some are auditory, language, nutritional, chemical, psychological, and motor-based. Behavioral optometry can be the missing link that helps address a learning difficulty using a multidisciplinary approach.

## Vision Testing Using a Developmental Approach

The doctor should first determine if the primitive reflexes have been inhibited. If they have not, then the more advanced motor skills, especially the fine motor skills (eye movements), will have a difficult time developing. Smooth eye movements are very important for learning to read easily.

The next test determines the relationship between eye movements and the inner ear. Balance is at play in the way eye movements and the vestibular system work together. Chronic ear infections can interfere with normal development of these two systems.

After these tests, the next evaluation of vision development is the twenty-one-point analytical examination. This examination gives the doctor information about the ocular motor system: how the child tracks, focuses, and coordinates the eyes. Determining how the child holds and controls eye muscles tells us about the muscle tone, not only of the eyes but of the entire body as well. If the eyes are flaccid (loose), then we want to determine how the rest of the body is holding. If the eyes are tight, then we want to see if the child's general motor development is also tight. Is he "muscling" his experience when using motor skills? Or are these motor skills automatically performed on a subconscious level?

Visual testing evaluates the flexibility of processing on a sensory-motor level. If there is a problem with visual input, then processing and output will be affected. This may be exhibited in the more advanced cognitive problem-solving skills such as spatial reasoning, visual memory, sequencing, and motor planning. The relationship between the right and left eye reflects processing on a cognitive brain level and an output/motor level. If the child's eyes are not working together, visually guiding or leading the movement with the eyes can be challenging. Problems with right and left can also be seen in the motor skills, such as skipping and jumping rope.

Dietary, metabolic, and immune issues also need to be addressed when behavior and learning problems exist. The key in this scenario is to treat the biochemical imbalance. After opening the detoxification pathways and improving digestive absorption, muscle tone, learning, and concentration will be better. This is a great time to recommend a holistic visual learning-thinking program, which helps the child learn how to use her sensory-motor system. It is done in a very sequential fashion so that true learning can take place.

## Vision Therapy

Once the vision imbalance is detected, vision therapy can help to improve the following visual-motor skills:

- General motor development, which includes bilateral integration, balance, rhythm, and timing
- Fine motor development, which includes visual tracking, visual focus, and visual coordination
- Hand-eye coordination

Vision therapy can also help to improve visual perceptual skills, including:

- Visual memory
- Form perception
- Spatial relationships
- Central-peripheral visual organization
- Visual-motor integration

If there are vision imbalances, vision therapy is a wonderful method to help the child reeducate his eyes, brain, and body to work together and process information more easily and with less stress. I have found many times that working with the primitive reflexes and gross motor development actually helps the fine motor visual skills (visual tracking, visual focusing, visual coordination abilities). Depending on the severity of the visual difficulty, the therapy continues an average of three to six months of weekly sixty-minute sessions.

Children today seem to be experiencing more and more breakdowns in their visual skills. One of the ways to ensure that the visual system supports proper learning is to have your preschool-age child tested by a behavioral/developmental optometrist before vision imbalances are evident. Researchers have shown that up to 80 percent of classroom learning takes place through the vision system. This is especially true in the early years of school. The earlier you can catch the problem, the easier it is to find a remedy.

It is far easier to practice prevention than to use a drug to control a hyperactive child, one who may get lost in the shuffle of a special education classroom or become a learning disabled adult. Vision is a learned and developed skill. It can be enhanced at any age. Vision therapy is a wonderful tool to help children become better learners!

## Brain Waves and Vision Therapy

Dr. William Ludlam of the College of Optometry in Vision Development tested visually evoked responses of children who had been diagnosed with visually related learning and concentration problems. The testing procedure was as follows: Flashing lights were shown into the children's eyes to measure how much information reached the cortex at the back of their brains. This process is similar to using an EEG biofeedback machine. Dr. Ludlam found that these children were not able to attenuate alpha waves. This means the children were not able to dampen these waves, which is critical for paying attention. After a program of vision therapy, Dr. Ludlam found that the children's alpha waves were normal and that they no longer had difficulty paying attention.[10]

## Lenses and Prisms

Lenses and prisms are also very important in developmental optometry, but these lenses are not prescribed to correct optical blur or acuity. They are prescribed with testing that is performed while the child is in the process of doing some dynamic task such as reading or focusing at his reading distance (measured from the child's knuckle to the elbow). Sometimes referred to as developmental low plus lenses, they can be used as a tool to help a child focus, to use peripheral vision more easily, and to process visual information with more efficiency.

I have observed these lenses acting as a catalyst to help the child connect her visual input with her brain and processing. The lens, when prescribed properly, will activate more of the retinal cells, which will then enable more of the brain to be engaged. The lenses are prescribed based on a dynamic focusing test. The child reads or focuses on a moving target as the doctor measures flexibility and response to the focusing by placing different preventive lenses over the eyes. These learning lenses allow more light into the eyes, which stimulates more of the retina and brain. They help retrain the visual system to see more with less effort and are generally worn six months to a year while the child is doing vision therapy. After the child begins to become visually efficient, in many cases the lenses won't be needed anymore.

The development lenses should be worn while the child is doing any kind of concentrated visual activity: reading, writing, doing mathematics, homework, studying, working on a computer, or watching television.

At Indiana University, John R. Pierce, O.D., Ph.D., replicated an interesting study concerning lenses and learning, which was originally conducted by Darrel Boyd Harmon at his radiological group in Austin, Texas. His study resulted in one of the most important educational films in use today. Low convex (plus) lenses were given to children and adults while they were reading. The lenses were given in small incremental increases. Photographs were taken to document the posture, working distance, and head tilt of each subject wearing the various lenses. Polygraphs documented the muscle activity in their back. Also measured and documented were the subjects' blood pressure, respiration, and galvanic skin response. When the optimum lens prescription was given, the subject's posture improved; tensions in the back were reduced (fewer nerve impulses were recorded); head and neck movements stopped; and blood pressure, respiratory rate, and galvanic skin conductivity returned to normal. Lenses that were too strong reversed these results. In other words, the wrong lenses were as detrimental as no lenses at all.[11] With the proper lenses, the subjects whose eyes were normal and free from disease saw 20/20 acuity at a distance and near.

Lenses and prisms are unique to developmental optometry. Some parents have said to me that these developmental lenses are "like Ritalin for the eyes" with no side effects.[12] The lenses can slow down a hyperactive child, improve his ability to focus and concentrate, and relax his visual-motor system.

## Important Aspects of Posture and Vision

The proper distance for all near activities should be twelve inches. Any distance closer creates more stress on the eyes, face, and neck muscles. This distance, named after Darrel Boyd Harmon, is called the

Harmon distance. It should be measured from the middle knuckle of the fist of either hand to the cheekbone of the face and allow the elbow of the arm to be placed on a page of a book or written material.

The optimal time period for all concentrated visual activities should be a maximum of fifty minutes, followed by a ten-minute break. If fifty minutes create stress, start with twenty-five-minute periods, followed by a five-minute break. Then gradually increase the period of study time until reaching the maximum of fifty minutes. Look up periodically at a distant object and blink to release visual stress.

The best place to study is in a quiet room with proper ventilation. Good lighting should consist of general room lighting and specific desk lighting from the right and left sides, which eliminates shadows on the work surface. A sloped posture board (20 degrees) should be used for all near activities. To enhance attention and reduce stimulation and distractions in the environment, a desk should be in a corner of a room or facing a wall, without visual distractions such as windows, mirrors, pictures, and so on. In school, the child's desk should be close to the teacher and the chalkboard. The average time a child should sit at a computer is thirty minutes. If a child is using a computer, it is important for him to get up and stretch and focus his eyes on a distant object. If a child is focusing on a computer for long periods of time, the visual-motor system is not being allowed to develop properly.

## Diet and Vision

The science of Ayurvedic medicine, which has been practiced in India for over four thousand years, says that diet influences the mind and that the mind, in turn, influences our choice of diet. When we eat in a balanced manner, we will be clear, peaceful, and joyful. The food that nourishes us is, of course, necessary for the whole body, but the eyes and brain, which comprise only 2 percent of the total body weight, use 25 percent of the body's nutrition.

Eating three balanced meals a day is not enough for many people. Biological stresses can affect our absorption of the food we eat. Hans Selye, who has extensively studied stress, found that a certain amount of stress—called eustress—is beneficial by causing change and growth. However, when stress becomes too great and becomes distress, it causes the person's system to break down. In today's world we are bombarded with many different types of stress: psychological stress, allergy overload, environmental toxicity, drug side effects, radiation, electromagnetic pollution, and negative thought patterns. These bombardments affect the endocrine, nervous, and immune systems, ultimately causing disease.

Generally, if a child can avoid food with refined sugars and artificial flavors, get enough essential fatty acids, and eat organic vegetables and complex carbohydrates, the eyes and the vision will remain clear and healthy.

## Syntonic Light Therapy

In my first year of optometry school, one of my instructors described the process by which light is refracted (bent) as it enters the eye and focuses on the retina. He stopped, however, at what happens to the light when it travels from the retina to the optic nerve and then to the brain. What happens is that 75 percent of the light that enters the eye continues on to the back of the brain, where the vision centers are located. The other 25 percent travels down the hypothalamic pathway to the hypothalamus, which is the regulator of both the autonomic nervous system (sympathetic and parasympathetic) and the endocrine system.

One part of the hypothalamus regulates the sympathetic nervous system, which increases hormonal output. The second part regulates the parasympathetic nervous system, which decreases hormonal output. As part of the central nervous system, the autonomic nervous system controls the internal actions of the body, such as heartbeat, breathing, and digestion. The sympathetic nervous system supports movement and action, and the parasympathetic nervous system works to rejuvenate and rebuild the body.

The hypothalamus both stimulates and inhibits hormonal function. It regulates secretions of the pituitary gland, thus affecting the body's hormonal functions. The hypothalamus is in constant communication with the glands and organs of the body. It regulates the energy balance, growth and maturation, circulation and breathing, emotions, reproduction, heat regulation activity, and sleep. It acts as the central conductor in controlling the life mechanisms in the body.

Another player in the regulation of the body's internal clock, one which is directly affected by light and color, is the pineal gland. Tucked beneath the brain, slightly above and behind the pituitary gland, this pea-sized organ "turns on" every night by releasing melatonin, a hormone that helps signal the body that it is time to sleep. The pineal gland's functioning is directly tied into the dark/light cycle. If we work the night shift, our body gets out of rhythm, and the dose of melatonin produced can leave us feeling depressed and lethargic.

Researchers are beginning to use light therapy introduced through the eyes to regulate the function of the nervous and endocrine systems of the body.[13] For example, light therapy is being used to turn off the pineal gland's production of melatonin in order to help people who work the night shift stay fully awake. Penn State University's Center for Cell Research, a NASA-funded center, and Dr. George Brainard, a neurologist at Jefferson Medical College in Philadelphia, have done a great deal of work with SAD (Seasonal Affective Disorder) using light therapy. Scientists are only beginning to scratch the surface of understanding how light affects our endocrine and nervous systems.

In the early 1930s, Dr. Harry Riley Spitler began to use light and color therapy directly on the eyes. Dr. Spitler, a medical doctor as well as an optometrist, conducted research leading to our understanding that different parts of the brain are directly related to the autonomic nervous system and the endocrine system. He also found that the eyes had the most direction connection through the nerve pathways to these two systems. Dr. Spitler devised methods of using light and color to balance the nervous system and improve visual processing. In 1933 he founded the College of Syntonic Optometry. Syntonics comes from the word *syntony*, which means "come back into balance." Today the College of Syntonic Optometry is dedicated to treating many different kinds of visual problems with colors projected directly into the eyes.

Dr. E. S. Edelman, a behavioral optometrist who practices in Newtown Square, Pennsylvania, has developed various protocols for working with adults and children suffering from AD/HD. First, Dr. Edelman has found that all people with AD/HD measure very small functional visual fields. When the visual fields are small, the peripheral vision is not being utilized. He has found that functional visual fields are directly affected by stress. The more stress, the smaller the visual fields. Diagnostic indicators are enlarged pupils, poor accommodative (visual focusing) responses, poor visual tracking, and poor visual coordination. Dr. Edelman has developed a protocol that helps to relax and rejuvenate the patient's nervous system by using different-colored lights on the eyes.

He has also seen a correlation between brain waves and color therapy. In his research, Dr. Edelman found that before using color therapy, the brain waves are beta only. During color treatment, the brain waves move into alpha and finally into theta wavelength. As the color treatments continue, his patients are able to control the brain waves better and operate more in the alpha wavelength range.

While this exciting work needs more research, the findings so far suggest that color and light therapy can be a helpful adjunct to other treatments for AD/HD.

## Auditory Integration Training

Listening is to hearing as vision is to eyesight. Listening is based on how well the ear can take in the sound and send it to the brain, where it is interpreted. Just as the eyes need to work together, the functions of both ears need to be coordinated. The vestibular system, which regulates certain types of eye movements, is also important to the processing of sound.

Some children with AD/HD have distortions or difficulty understanding what they hear. If a child has had chronic fluid in her ears caused by ear infections, it will be challenging for her to learn how to use her ears, and this can cause difficulty with her ability to distinguish sounds. Many times children can hear sounds but have an inconsistency with hearing different frequencies. Also, both ears will have a problem working together. The brain will be confused while trying to sort out the sounds, and this can result in behaviors such as distractibility, inattentiveness, or hyperactivity.

There are several types of auditory improvement programs offered today, which all use specialized electronic equipment. The procedure entails having a person listen to music that is specifically modified and filtered to meet the person's needs based on an initial audiogram of his hearing. This music program activates the vestibular system, which, in turn, stimulates the language centers of the brain, eye movements, and the digestive system. In working with the whole child, auditory training can be an effective piece to the child's puzzle.

Another approach to auditory training involves the work of Don Campbell, the author of *The Mozart Effect: Tapping the Power of Music to Heal the Body, Strengthen the Mind and Unlock the Creative Spirit.* Campbell believes that music is a dietary need for proper childhood development. He describes the organ of hearing as being important for balance and time/space perception. Campbell says that hearing teaches a child how to communicate, speak, sing, and dance. He draws from the work of Alfred Tomatis, a French physician, who believes that faulty listening is the underlying cause of many learning difficulties. Making a distinction between hearing and listening, he says that hearing is the passive ability to receive auditory information through the ears, skin, and bone; while listening is the active ability to filter, focus on, remember, and respond to sound. Listening well creates a range of positive effects, including more energy, a better disposition, and improved vocal control, handwriting, and posture.

Children with listening disorders may have speech impediments, poor motor coordination, and difficulties in standing, sitting, crawling, or walking. Tomatis found that listening or learning problems could be corrected by improving the control of the muscles of the middle ear, where distinctions between listening and hearing begin.

Campbell says that Mozart's music is in the high-frequency range and that these frequencies help to activate the brain and increase attention. The Tomatis method relies on filtered high-frequency recordings of the Gregorian chants.

Campbell recommends the following: On your sound system, lower the bass and the midrange and raise the treble. Music with violins will give you the best results. Frequencies from 2,000 through 8,000 hertz produce the greatest charge. The right ear should be directed toward the speaker. He also recommends listening to Mozart in half-hour doses, and that children make their own music using drums or simple instruments.

Any sensory-processing therapies should include the occupational therapist as an important facilitator to help a child learn to guide his body to respond to sensory input. The more a child is able to respond to sensory challenges, the better he will be able to learn and problem solve. Helping children with AD/HD takes a multidisciplinary approach with professionals working together holistically.

## Homeopathy and Cell Salts

Dr. Samuel Hahnemann, M.D., a German physician, invented homeopathy over two hundred years ago. Using the laws of similars, which means "like cures like," a small dosage of a remedy is given to stimulate the body's immune system to heal itself.[14] Homeopathic remedies, derived from plants, animals, or mineral substances, are safe and cause no side effects. They are very effective for babies and small children and work extremely well if the underlying cause of a physical problem is emotionally based. Once symptoms have been alleviated, the remedy can be discontinued. The basis of homeopathy is that it treats the whole person, not the symptoms, by stimulating the body's own healing blueprint to take over and balance the body.

The symptoms a person exhibits are the body's best attempt to reestablish its own natural balance. Symptoms are like an alarm clock going off. Instead of turning off the alarm by treating the symptoms with drugs such as Ritalin, why not look at what has caused the alarm to go off in the first place? When we are just treating symptoms, we are driving the problem further into the body, and the imbalance becomes more embedded.

Homeopathy works this way: If a healthy person is given a large quantity of a natural substance, it will cause symptoms. On the other hand, a small quantity of a natural substance will stimulate a person's immune system.[15] Say, for example, you peel an onion, and your eyes itch, burn, and water; you might sneeze and have a runny nose. The symptoms of a cold, with runny nose, watery eyes, and sneezing, are similar. If you take a dose of a homeopathic remedy, which is a small amount of the effective substance simulating an onion, the remedy will stimulate the body to heal itself.

Homeopathy works by treating the whole body, including body, mind, and spirit. Very tiny doses are given to create a gentle response in the person. Homeopathy helps people connect to their own healing powers and immune systems. The remedies (medicines) are prepared from natural substances. These substances cause various symptoms in a healthy person but can cure the same symptoms in a sick person by stimulating the body's ability to heal itself. As an example, ipecac is given in large quantities to induce vomiting but, if given in minute dosages, it stops vomiting.[16]

Hundreds of studies have documented the effectiveness of homeopathy. In France, homeopatic remedies are dispensed by most pharmacies, with one-third of all physicians integrating it into their practice.[17] In Germany, 20 percent of physicians use homeopathic remedies.[18] In India, 55 percent of medical doctors use it.[19] And homeopathy is an essential component used in the practice of holistic medicine.

## Common AD/HD Symptoms and Homeopathic Remedies[20]

| Remedy | Disorder |
| --- | --- |
| Anacardium | bizarre convictions or fear of being followed |
| Arsenicum album | hyperactivity, allergies |
| Baryta carbonica | developmental delays |
| Cannabis | autism |
| Capsicum | irritability, anger |
| Carcinosin | dull mind, disinterest in conversation |
| Chamomile | bad temper, impatience, frustration |
| Cina | restlessness, fidgeting |
| Helleborus | history of encephalitis or head injury |
| Hyoscyamus | impulsivity |
| Lachesis | jealousy, sarcasm |
| Lycopodium | dictatorial, bossy, fearful actions |
| Medorrhinum | fear of public places |
| Nux vomica | irritability leading to rage |
| Platina | arrogance, contemptuousness |
| Stramonium | fear of death, the dark, dogs, evil, abandonment |
| Sulphur | fear of being bathed |
| Tarantula hispanica | restlessness, hyperactivity |
| Tuberculinum | destructiveness, maliciousness with violence and anger |
| Veratrum album | repetitive behavior, hyperactivity |

## What Are Cell Salts?

Dr. W. H. Schuessler, through his research, found that taking mineral salts could help reverse imbalances and diseases people suffer when these minerals are missing in the tissues of their bodies. He discovered twelve such mineral salts, which he called cell salts. His research found that certain symptoms indicated that certain cell salts were missing in the body. When the proper cell salts were added, the body's own immune system was stimulated to heal itself. According to Dr. Schuessler, the twelve cell salts contain all the ingredients of traditional homeopathic remedies. Cell salts simplify prescribing homeopathic medicine. These salts exist in rocks, the earth, soil, vegetation, our food, and the mineral hot springs in which we soak.

Cell salts are an effective and inexpensive method of helping the body rebalance itself. For children with attention and concentration problems, cell salts used in the proper dosage and combinations can be helpful in reducing symptoms and bringing the body back into balance. The key is linking the appropriate cell salt combinations with the symptoms, which are signals that tell what the body needs. When the body's cell salts are balanced, the organs, glands, and tissues will work at their optimal level. The key is finding out what and where symptoms exist in the body and using the appropriate cell salts to rebalance the body.

The dosage and frequency of taking cell salts are very important in using them for treatment. They are most effective when the tablets are placed under the tongue and allowed to dissolve. This assures that the cell salts bypass the stomach and go directly to the area of the body that needs healing. Never touch the tablets with your fingers, instead, use a clean spoon to remove them from the bottle and place them under the tongue.

Cell salts are safe and nonaddictive, produce no side effects, and don't interfere with any other medications. When giving cell salts, do so for a week or so, even after the symptoms are gone.

## Common AD/HD Symptoms and Cell Salt Treatments[21]

| Remedy | Disorder |
| --- | --- |
| Calcium fluoride | tension in muscles, slowed development |
| Calcium phosphate | impaired memory, slow comprehension |
| Calcium sulphate | irritability, moodiness |
| Ferrum phosphate | tics in the face, feeling discouraged |
| Kali mur | suggishness, lowered immunity |
| Magnesium phosphate | depression, sleeplessness, nervousness, poor concentration |
| Potassium chloride | sluggishness, lowered immunity |
| Potassium phosphate | crying, anxious moods, fidgety, impatient, ill tempered, screaming, nervous exhaustion |
| Potassium sulphate | obstinance |
| Silica oxide | agitation, poor attention |
| Sodium chloride | anger, crying, excessive talking |
| Sodium phosphate | nervousness, depression, anger |
| Sodium sulphate | obstinance, discouragement |

## Structural Therapies

Structural therapies realign the body's internal parts. The structural and skeletal systems of the body affect the organs, fluids, bones, and connective tissues. Many of the symptoms children experience from AD/HD can be alleviated from structural therapies, with the digestive and nervous systems being particularly affected. Manipulation of a specific area of the body activates its own healing system to bring its function back into balance. Osteopathic physicians, health professionals trained in craniosacral techniques, massage therapists, and chiropractors can offer gentle, restorative manipulation to bring the body back into balance.

Researchers in the *Journal of the Osteopathic Association* reported that children with AD/HD who received osteopathic manipulation showed reduced symptoms and improved neurological development. Manipulation therapy also helped reduce the incidence of ear infections and upper respiratory infections.[22]

The Upledger Institute reported that craniosacral therapists have been able to take stress and pressure off the brain stem, which helps with neurological development.[23] Therefore, children diagnosed with developmental delays can begin to improve their sensory-motor developmental skills, which are necessary for learning. Also reported by the Upledger Institute was a reduction in vision problems such as nystagmus, strabismus, and glaucoma. But probably the institute's most exciting finding was that its craniosacral therapists have been able to help children with allergies to make dietary changes.

## Essential Oils

Essential oils are a branch of herbal medicine. According to Dr. Kurt Schnaubelt, director of the Pacific Institute of Aromatherapy, essential oils, which come from leaves, branches, and roots of plants, are effective because their small molecular size easily penetrates the skin.[24] Essential oils are effective for treating the adrenal glands, ovaries, and thyroid gland; they help energize, pacify, detoxify, and generally have a positive effect on the nervous system, immune system, digestive system, and the emotional body.

John Steele, Ph.D., of Sherman Oaks, California, and Robert Tisserand of London, England, have studied the effects of aromatherapy and essential oils on brain waves.[25] They have found that oils such as orange, jasmine, and rose give a brain wave alpha rhythm that enhances calmness and tranquility; and essential oils such as basil, black pepper, cardamon, and rosemary produce heightened responses (a beta rhythm response).[26] Essential oils can help reduce negative thought patterns and increase intuitive thoughts.

Essential oils can be administered in four ways.

1. A diffusor disperses very small particles of the oils into the air and can help respiratory conditions.
2. Oils can be rubbed directly on the body, added to baths, mixed with hot oil for massage, and used in cold compresses.
3. The oil may be sprayed into the air with a sprayer.
4. Essential oils may be taken internally, although this approach should always be under the supervision of a qualified health professional.

One of the easiest ways to receive the benefits of essential oils is through our sense of smell. The olfactory senses activate brain chemistry, and the essential oils affect the limbic system of the brain, which controls a person's emotions and memory. The odor stimulation causes many neurotransmitters to be released in the brain. Serotonin, one such neurotransmitter, promotes relaxation and sleep. Endorphins, another neurotransmitter, can help ease pain and promote euphoria.

Essential oils have also been used in Egypt, Italy, India, China, and France to treat a variety of conditions. In England, essential oils are used primarily for stress-related issues. Nurses on hospital staffs use essential oil massages to relieve pain and to induce sleep. Essential oils are used to relieve stress associated with cancer and AIDS. Hospitals in England use essential oils vaporized to combat infectious diseases. Essential oils have also been used topically as antiseptics in creams and skin ointments and in liniments for arthritic pain. In general, essential oils are used as medicines to kill bacteria, viruses, and fungi. The fragrances are used to balance moods, release negative emotions, and increase oxygen supply to glands and organs. They can help bring more oxygen to the body.

Buying essential oils can be confusing, and they also can be expensive because, according to Dr. Kurt Schnaubelt, it takes one thousand pounds of plant material to produce just one pound of essence.

## AD/HD and Essential Oils

In a paper presented at a conference in 1998 by F. Hadji-Minaglou, a pharmacist from Grasse, France, it was resolved that certain essential oils in a diffused vaporizer helped to improve memory and concentration, reduced stress, and showed a CNS (central nervous system) rebalancing effect. Children were happier, calmer, and better able to relax.[27] While more research needs to be done in this area, essential oils can be an effective adjunct to other AD/HD treatments.

Essential oils that help to improve memory, concentration, and fatigue include basil, rosemary, peppermint, and lemon. Those that help to relieve insomnia, stress, and anxiety include marjoram, neroli, lavender, and chamomile. Essential oils used to reduce AD/HD behaviors include lavender, sandalwood, cardamom, basil, frankincense, and melissa. These oils also have been effective for helping those with autism and developmental delays.

Dr. Samuel A. Berne offers certification courses on Vision Development and Learning to occupational therapists, special education teachers, other professionals, and parents. His schedule may be found on his Web site at www.Vision-enhancement.com or contact his office at:

227 East Palace Avenue, Suite G
Santa Fe, NM 87501
Phone: (505) 984-2030
Fax: (505) 984-1082

# Notes and Other References

## Introduction

1. Thomas D. Schram, "The Eyes Have It in Attention Disorder: Visual Focus May Be Affecting Mental Focus," *HealthSCOUT Reporter*, 20 April 1999, 1.

2. Ibid., 2.

3. "Eye Exams to Uncover Vision Disorders in Children That Affect Learning Are Recommended," *Medscape* 2 (May 2000), URL: NEWS @medpulse.medscape.com.

## Chapter 1

1. Peter Breggin, *War Against Children* (New York: St. Martin's Press, 1996), 76.

2. Judith Reichenberg and Robert Ullman, *Ritalin-Free Kids* (Rockland, Calif.: Prima Publishing, 1996), 37.

3. Ibid.

4. Erica Goode, "Sharp Rise in Psychiatric Drugs for the Very Young," *New York Times*, 29 February 2000, 45.

5. R. A. Barkley, "The Adolescent Outcome of Hyperactive Children Diagnosed by Research Criteria I: An 8-year Prospective Follow-up Study," *Journal of the American Academy of Child and Adolescent Psychiatry* 29, no. 4 (July 1990): 546–56.

6. "Misuses of Ritalin by School Children Prompts Warning," *Seattle Times*, 27 March 1996, 3.

7. "Boom in Ritalin Sales Raise Ethical Issues," *New York Times*, 15 May 1966, 17.

## Other Sources

Biederman, Joseph, et al. "Diagnoses of Attention-Deficit Disorder from Parent Reports Predict Diagnosis Based on Teachers Reports." *Journal of the American Academy of Child and Adolescent Psychiatry* 32, no. 20 (March 1995): 315–22.

Hallowell, Edward, and John Ratey. *Driven to Distraction: Recognizing and Coping with Attention Deficit Disorder from Childhood Through Adulthood.* New York: Simon and Schuster, 1994.

P.A.V.E. Pamphlet. "The Hidden Disability: Undetected Vision Problems." November 1991.

Zametkin, Alan. "Attention-Deficit Disorder: Born to Be Hyperactive?" *Journal of the American Medical Association* 273, no. 23 (21 June 1995): 1871–74.

Zimmerman, Marcia. *The A.D.D. Nutrition Solution.* New York: Henry Holt & Co., 1999.

## Chapter 2

1. R. A. Barkley et al., "Side Effects of Methylphenidate in Children with Attention Deficit-Hyperactivity Disorder: A Systemic, Placebo-Controlled Evaluation," *Pediatrics* 86, no. 2 (August 1990): 184–92.

2. Erica Goode, "Sharp Rise in Psychiatric Drugs for the Very Young," *New York Times*, 29 February 2000, 46.

3. Gretchen LeFever, Keila Dawson, and Ardythe Morrow, "The Extent of Drug Therapy for Attention Deficit-Hyperactivity Disorder Among Children in Public Schools," *American Journal of Public Health* 89, no. 9 (September 1999): 1359–63.

4. Harold S. Koplewica, "The Role for Pills in Preschool," *New York Times*, 1 March 2000, 10.

5. Ibid.

6. Erica Goode, "Fury, Not Facts, in the Battle over Childhood Behavior," *New York Times*, 3 March 2000, 46.

7. Ibid., 47.

8. Judith Reichenberg and Robert Ullman, *Ritalin-Free Kids* (Rockland, Calif.: Prima Publishing, 1996), xv.

9. "Misuses of Ritalin," 4.

10. Peter Breggin, *War Against Children*, 59.

## Other Sources

Barkley, R. A. "A Review of Stimulant Drug Research with Hyperactive Children." *Journal of Child Psychology and Psychiatry* 18 (1997): 137–65.

Block, Mary Ann. *No More Ritalin: Testing ADHD Without Drugs.* New York: Kensington Books, 1996.

Gentieu, Penny. "Kids and Pills." *USA Weekend Edition*, 27–29 October 1995.

Rappley, Marsh. "Safety Issued in the Use of Methylphenidate." *Drug Safety* 17, no. 3 (September 1997): 143–48.

Robbins, John. *Reclaiming Our Health.* Tiburon, Calif.: H. J. Kramer, 1996.

# Chapter 4

1. Ira Schwartz and Abe Shapiro, eds., *The Collected Works of Lawrence W. Macdonald, O.D., vol. 2, 1968–1979* (Santa Ana, Calif.: OEP Publishing, 1993), 44.

2. Arnold Gesell, Francis Ilg, and Garry Bullis, *Vision: Its Development in Infant and Child* (Santa Ana, Calif.: OEP Publishing, 1998), 37.

3. Hollie McHugh, "Auditory and Vestibular Disorders in Children" (paper presented at the meeting of the Eastern Section, American Laryngological, Rhinological, and Otological Society, N.Y., January 1962).

## Other Sources

Baxstrom, Curtis. "Vestibulo-Optokinetic Interactions in the Development of Binocularity and Strabismus." Paper presented at 40th Annual Invitation Skeffington Symposium, January 1995.

Berne, Samuel A. "Vestibular Insufficiency Syndrome." Lecture at the Skeffington Symposium, Washington, D.C., January 2000.

Goddard, Sally. *A Teacher's Window into the Child's Mind.* Eugene, Ore.: Fern Ridge Press, 1996.

Gold, Svea J. "Attention Deficit Syndrome: Educational Bugaboo of the '90s" (5 March 1995): 1–10.

Hyabach, P. J. "Scientists Explore ANS/Vestibular Links." *Journal of Vestibular Research* (January/February 1998): 56–60.

La Poncin, Monique. *Brain Fitness.* New York: Fawcett Columbine, 1990, 115–120.

Lisberger, Stephen G. "Neural Bases for Learning of Simple Motor Skills." *Science* 242 (4 November 1988): 728–35.

Ludlam, William. "Visual Electrophysiology and Reading/Learning Difficulties." *Journal of the American Optometric Association*, December 1981, 29.

Nilsson, Lennart. *A Child Is Born*. New York: Delacorte Press, 1978.

Ratcliffe, Norman A., and Andrew F. Rowley. "The Development of Human Fetal-Eye Movement Patterns." *Science* 213 (August 1981): 679.

Reuterhall, Lena, and Thorkild Rasmussen. "Residual Primitive Reflexes." Lecture given in Miami, Fla., October 2000.

Rhodes, Christopher P. "The Retina of the Newborn Human Infant," *Science* 217 (July 1982): 265–66.

Robbins, John. *Reclaiming Our Health*. Tiburon, Calif.: H. J. Kramer, 1996.

Sutton, Albert A. "The Basis for Visual Development from Prenatal Through Infancy." *Journal of Optometric Vision Development*, (Summer 1986): 51.

———. *Vision Intelligence Creativity*. Santa Ana, Calif.: OEP Publishing, 1988.

———. "Development of Vision-Learning-Thinking Through Life." Seminar in Santa Fe, N.M., February 2000, 5.

Yate, B. M., and S. D. Miller. *Vestibular Autonomic Regulation*. Boca Raton, Fla.: CRC Press, 1996.

## Chapter 5

1. Patricia S. Lemer, "Treatments for Those on the Autistic Spectrum," *Journal of Behavioral Optometry* 9, no. 2 (1988): 143–49.

2. Jeffrey Bland and Sara H. Benum, *The 20-Day Rejuvenation Diet Program* (Los Angeles: Keats, 1996), 88.

3. Lemer.

4. Ibid.

5. Bland, *20-Day Rejuvenation Diet*, 88.

## Other Sources

Arky, Ronald. *Physician's Desk Reference*. Oradell, N.J.: Medical Economics, 1998.

Galland, Leo. *Power Healing*. New York: Random House, 1997.

Gillberg, C. "Amphetamines Can Provide Long-Term Benefit in Treatment of ADHD." *American Journal of Psychiatric Medicine*, September 1997.

Knonpasek, D. E. *Medication Fact Sheets: A Medication Reference Guide for the Non-Medical Professional*. Anchorage, Alaska: Arctic Term Publishing, 1997.

Swanson, J. M. "Effect of Stimulant Medication on Children with Attention Deficit Disorder, A Review of Reviews." *Exceptional Children* (1993): 154–62.

# Chapter 6

1. Dr. James Rouse, "Metagenics Now: News on the Wire," 30 June 2000. *www.metagenics.com*

2. Marcia Zimmerman. *The A.D.D. Nutrition Solution*, (New York, Henry Holt & Co.), 54.

3. Ibid., 139.

4. Ibid., 24.

5. Skye Weintraub. *Natural Treatments for ADD and Hyperactivity* (Pleasant Grove, Utah: Woodland Publishing), 190.

6. R. W. Tuthill, "Hair Lead Levels Related to Children's Classroom Attention-Defecit Behavior," *Archives of Environmental Health* 51(3) (May/June 1996): 214.

7. Weintraub, *Natural Treatments*, 191.

8. Weintraub, *Natural Treatments*, 190.

9. Tuthill, "Hair Levels," 215.

10. Weintraub, *Natural Treatments*, 187.

11. Peggy O'Mara, "Vaccination: The Issue of Our Times," *Mothering Magazine Publishing* (Santa Fe, N.M.: 1997), 7.

12. Bernard Rimland, "Vaccines: Major Medical Political Developments Fuel Furor over Vaccines," *Autism Research Reviews* 13, no. 3 (1999): 4.

13. O'Mara, "Vaccination: The Issue of Our Times," 15.

14. Randi J. Hagerman and Alice R. Falkenstein, "An Association Between Recurrent Otitis Media in Infancy and Later Hyperactivity," *Clinical Pediatrics* (May 1987): 253.

15. Michael A. Schmidt, *Healing Childhood Ear Infections* (Berkeley: North Atlantic Books, 1997), 11.

16. Ibid., 60.

17. Zimmerman, *The A.D.D. Solution*, 100.

18. Mary Ann Block, *No More Ritalin*, 76.

19. Bonnie Spring, P. J. Wurtman, and J. J. Wurtman, eds., "Effects of Foods and Nutrients on the Behavior of Normal Individuals," *Nutrients and the Brain* (September 1986): 45.

## Other Sources

Crook, William G. *Yeast and How They Can Make You Sick.* Jackson, Tenn.: Professional Books, 1997.

Dipenza, Joseph. *Live Better Longer: The Parcells Center 7-Step Plan for Health and Longevity.* San Francisco: Harper, 1997.

Dorfman, Kelly. "10 Trends in Treating Children with Learning, Attentional, and Behavioral Issues." Lecture at St. Columbia's, Washington, D.C., March 1999.

Kaplan, Sheila, and Jim Morris. "Kids at Risk." *U.S. News and World Report*, 19 June 2000, 47–53.

Raloff, J. "Picturing Pesticides' Impact on Kids." *Science News* 153 (6 June 1998): 358.

Rimland, Bernard. "Nutritional and Ecological Approaches to the Reduction of Criminality, Delinquency and Violence," *Journal of Applied Nutrition* 33, no. 2 (1981): 116–37.

# Chapter 7

1. Skye Weintraub, *Natural Treatments for ADD and Hyperactivity* (Pleasant Grove, Utah: Woodland Publishing), 133.

2. T. M. Nsouli and S. M. Nsouli, "The Role of Food Allergy in Serous Otitis Media," *Annals of Allergy* 73, no. 3 (September 1994): 215.

3. A. Lucas et al., "Breast Milk and Subsequent Intelligence Quotient in Children Born Preterm," *Lancet* 339 (1992): 261–64.

4. J. R. Burgess et al., "Essential Fatty Acid Metabolism in Boys with ADHD," *American Journal of Clinical Nutrition* 62 (1995): 761–68.

5. Ibid., 762.

6. L. J. Stevens et al., "Omega 3 Fatty Acid in Boys with Behavior, Learning, and Health Problems," *Physiological Behavior* 59, nos. 4–5 (1996): 915–20.

7. E. A. Mitchell et al., "Clinical Characteristics and Serum Essential Fatty Acid Levels in Hyperactive Children," *Clinical Pediatrics* 26 (1987): 406–11.

8. Ibid., 409.

9. Stevens et al., "Omega 3 Fatty Acid."

10. C. L. Lanting et al., "Neurological Differences Between 9-Year-Old Children Fed Breast-Milk or Formula-Milk as Babies," *Lancet* 344 (1994): 1319–22.

11. Anonymous, "Organochlorines Laced Inuit Breast Milk," *Science News*, 13 February 1994.

12. Ralph Holman, Sid Johnson, and Paul Ogburn, "Deficiency of Essential Fatty Acids and Membrane Fluidity During Pregnancy and Lactation," *National Academy Science Journal*, no. 88 (1991): 4835–39.

13. Monique Al, "The Effect of Pregnancy in Cervonic Acid," (paper presented at International Congress of International Society of Study of Fatty Acids and Lipids, Washington, D.C., June 1995), 3.

## Other Sources

Anderson, Nina. *ADD, The Natural Approach*. East Canaan, Conn.: Safe Goods, 1996.

Baker, Sidney. "Environmental Medicine: Comprehensive, Case Oriented, and Preventive Care." Paper presented at American Academy of Environmental Medicine Symposium, Dearborn, Mich., 1996.

Braly, James. *Dr. Braly's Food Allergy and Nutrition Revolution*. New Canaan, Conn.: Keats, 1992.

Crawford, Michael. "The Role of Essential Fatty Acids in Neural Development: Implications for Prenatal Nutrition." *American Journal of Clinical Nutrition Supplement* (1993): 703S–10S.

Egger, Joseph. "Psychoneurological Aspects of Food Allergy." *European Journal of Clinical Nutrition* 45, supp. 1 (1991): 35–45.

Gaby, Alan. "The Role of Hidden Food Allergy/Intolerance in Chronic Disease." *Alternative Medical Reviews* 3, no.2 (April 1998): 90–100.

Gibbs, Nancy, "The Age of Ritalin," *Time*, 30 November 1986, 33.

Hoffman, Dennis, et al. "Effects of Supplementation with Long Chain Polyunsaturated Fatty Acids on Retinal and Cortical Development in Premature Infants." *American Journal of Clinical Nutrition* 57, supp. (1993): 807S–12S.

Marshall, Paul. "Attention Deficit Disorder and Allergy: A Neuro-chemical Model of the Relation Between the Illnesses." *Psychological Bulletin* 106, no. 3 (March 1989): 434–46.

McGee, R., W. R. Stanton, and M. R. Sears. "Allergic Disorders and Attention Deficit Disorder in Children," *Journal of Abnormal Child Psychology* 23, no. 1 (1993): 79–88.

O'Shea, J. A., and S. F. Porter. "Double-Blind Study Reconfirms Link Between Allergens and Some Hyperkinetics." *Journal of Learning Disabilities* 14 (1998): 189–91.

Philpott, William, and Dwight Kalita. *Brain Allergies: The Psychonutrient Connection*. New Canaan, Conn.: Keats, 1980.

Rapp, Doris J., *Allergies and Your Family*. New York: Sterling Publishing Company, 1989.

———. *Is This Your Child?* New York: William Morrow, Quill Books, 1991.

Rogers, Sherry, *Depression Cured at Last*. Sarasota, Fla.: SK Publishing, 1997.

Rowe, K. S., and K. J. Rowe, "Synthetic Food Coloring and Behavior: A Dose Response Effect in a Double-Blind Placebo-Controlled, Repeated Measures Study." *Journal of Pediatrics* 125 (1994): 691–98.

Schmidt, Michael A. *Smart Fats: How Dietary Fats and Oils Affect Mental, Physical, and Emotional Intelligence*. Berkeley: Frog Ltd., 1997.

Smith, Lendon. *Foods for Healthy Kids*. New York: Berkeley Books, 1981.

Stevens, Laura J., and Sydney S. Zentall. "Essential Fatty Acid Metabolism in Boys with Attention-Deficiency Hyperactivity Disorder." *American Journal of Clinical Nutrition* 62 (1995): 761–68.

## Chapter 8

1. Naomi Aldort, "Getting Out of the Way." *Parabola* (June 1998): 11.

2. Arnold Gesell, Francis Ilg, and Carry Bullis, *Vision: Its Development in Infant and Child* (Santa Ana, Calif.: OEP Publishing, 1998), 25.

3. Hans Furth and Harry Wachs, *Piaget's Theory in Practice: Thinking Goes to School* (New York: Oxford University Press, 1975), 12.

4. Albert Sutton, "Development of Vision-Learning-Thinking Through Life," 14.

5. Richard Kavenar, *Your Child's Vision* (New York: Simon and Schuster, 1985), 28.

6. Kenneth Lane, *Developing Your Child for Success* (Lewisville, Tex.: Potentials Publishers, 1991), 2.

7. Lee Carroll and Jan Tober, *The Indigo Children* (Carlsbad, Calif.: Hay House, 1999), 45–47.

8. Albert Sutton, "Vision Intelligence Creativity" (Santa Ana, Calif.: OEP Publishing, 1988), 25.

### Other Sources

Ayres, Jean. *Sensory Integration and the Child.* Los Angeles: Western Psychological Services, 1998.

Beery, Keith. *Revised Administration, Scoring, and Teaching Manual for the Developmental Test of Visual-Motor Integration.* Modern Curriculum Press, 1981.

Berne, Samuel A. *Creating Your Personal Vision: A Mind-Body Guide for Better Eyesight.* Santa Fe, N.M.: Colorstone Press, 1994.

Campbell, Don. *The Mozart Effect: Tapping the Power of Music to Heal the Body, Strengthen the Mind, and Unlock the Creative Spirit.* New York: William Morrow and Company, 2000.

Corballis, Michael, and Ivan Beale. *The Ambivalent Mind.* Chicago: Nelson-Hall, 1983.

DeQuiros, Julio, and Orlando Schrager. "Neuropsychological Fundamentals in Learning Disabilities." *Academic Therapy Publications* (1997): 39.

Frankenburg, William, and Josiah Dobbs. "Denver Developmental Screen Test." University of Colorado Medical Center, 1988.

Ginsburg, Oppers H. *Piaget's Theory of Intellectual Development.* New York: Prentice Hall, 1969.

Reuterhall, Lena, and Thorkild Rosmussen. "Residual Primitive Reflexes." Lecture given in Miami, Fla., October 2000.

Richter, Eileen W., and Patricia Montgomery. *The Sensorimotor Performance Analysis.* Hugo, Minn.: PDP Press, 1989.

# Chapter 9

1. George Pavlidis, "Two-Year Study on Dyslexia," *Education of the Handicap Journal* (1 October 1986): 15.

2. "The Works of A. M. Skeffington," *Infant and Toddler Strabismus and Amblyopia Behavioral Aspects of Vision Care 2000,* ed. Ann Barber, vol. 41, no. 2 (Santa Ana, Calif.: OEP Publications, 2000), 67.

3. Albert Sutton, "Development of Vision-Learning-Thinking Through Life," 45.

4. Kenneth C. Koslowe, "Optometric Services in Reading Disability Clinic Initial Results," *Journal of Behavioral Optometry* 6 (1995): 67–68.

5. Martin H. Birnbaum, "Vision Disorders Frequently Interfere with Reading and Learning: They Should Be Diagnosed and Treated," *Journal of Behavioral Optometry* 4 (1993): 66–71.

6. Gary Sigler and Todd Wylie, "The Effect of Vision Therapy on Reading and Vision Disorders," *Journal of Behavioral Optometry* 5, no. 3 (1994): 63–67.

7. Mitchell Scheiman, "Scotopic Sensitivity Syndrome Reading Disability and Vision Disorders," *Journal of Behavioral Optometry* 5, no. 3 (1994): 63–67.

8. Lut Helsen and W. C. Maples, "The Optometric Evaluation of Adult Females Who Are Participating in a Remedial Reading Program," *Journal of Behavioral Optometry* 5, no. 4 (1994): 87–90.

9. Stanley Kaseno, "The Visual Anatomy of Juvenile Delinquency," *Academic Therapy* (September 1985): 5.

10. William Ludlam, "Visual Electrophysiology and Reading/Learning Difficulties." *American Journal of Optometry and Psychological Optics* 5, no. 10 (October 1985): 571.

11. John Pierce, "A Study of the Relationship Between Performance and Physiological Activity as a Function of Near Point Working Distance and Posture" (Ph.D. diss., University of Portland, 1970), 162.

12. Patricia S. Lemer, "Treatments for Those on the Autistic Spectrum," *Journal of Behavioral Optometry* 9, no. 2 (1988):148.

13. Samuel A. Berne, *Creating Your Personal Vision: A Mind-Body Guide for Better Eyesight* (Santa Fe, N.M.: Colorstone Press, 1994), 158.

14. Burton Goldberg et al., *Alternative Medicine: The Definitive Guide* (Tiburon, Calif.: The Burton Goldberg Group, Future Medicine Publishing, 1995), 273.

15. D. T. Riley et al., "Is Homeopathy a Placebo Response? Controlled Trial of Homeopathic Potency with Pollen in Hayfever as a Model," *Lancet* (18 October 1996): 55.

16. D. T. Riley, "Is Evidence of Homeopathy Reproduced?" *Lancet* (1994): 334.

17. Moessinger, "Zur Behandlung der Otitis Media mit Pulsatilla," *Allegemeine Homoopathische* 230 (1985): 89.

18. J. Jacobs, "The Efficacy of Homeopathic Medicines on Diarrhea," *Journal of the American Pediatric Association* (February 1994): 220.

19. Schmidt, *Healing Childhood Ear Infections.*

20. Weintraub, *Natural Treatments*, 244.

21. Ibid., 245.

22. Ida Schmidt, "Osteopathic Manipulative Therapy as a Primary Factor in the Management of Upper, Middle, and Para Respiratory Infections," *Journal of the American Osteopathic Association* 81, no. 6 (February 1982): 382–88.

23. V. Frymann et al., "Effect of Osteopathic Medical Management on Neurological Development in Children," *Journal of the American Osteopathic Association* 92, no. 6 (June 1992): 729–44.

24. Goldberg et al., *Alternative Medicine: The Definitive Guide*, 53.

25. John Steele and Robert Tisserand, "Brain Research and Essential Oils," *Aromatherapy Quarterly* 3 (spring 1984): 21; *The Art of Aromatherapy* (Rochester, Vt.: Healing Arts Press, 1977), 76.

26. Steele, "Brain Research," 22.

27. F. Hadji-Minaglou, "ADHD in Children Phytoaromatherapy, An Alternative to Ritalin," *Essential Science* (March 2000): 68.

## Other Sources

Apell, Richard, and Ray Loury. *Preschool Vision*. St. Louis: American Optometric Association, 1959.

Berne, Samuel A. *Creating Your Personal Vision: A Mind-Body Guide for Better Eyesight*. Santa Fe, N.M.: Colorstone Press, 1994.

Campbell, Dan. *The Mozart Effect: Tapping the Power of Music to Heal the Body, Strengthen the Mind, and Unlock the Creative Spirit*. New York: William Morrow & Co., 2000.

Cardinal, Donald, Garth N. Christenson, and John R. Griffin. "The Neurological-Behavioral Model of Dyslexia." *Journal of Behavioral Optometry* 3, no. 2 (1992): 35–39.

Edelman, Ellis. "Nonmalingering Syndrome." Lecture given at Syntonic Optometry Conference, Niagara Falls, N.Y., May 2001.

Eriksen, Marlene. *Healing with Aromatherapy*. Los Angeles: Keats Publishing, 2000.

Essential Science Publishing, comp. *PDR for Essential Oils*. Salem, Utah: Science Publishing, 1999.

Forrest, Elliot. *Stress and Vision*. Santa Ana, Calif.: OEP Publishing, 1988.

Gerhard, W. "The Biological Treatment of Migraines Based on Experience." *Biological Therapy* 5, no. 3 (June 1998): 67–71.

Hoorigan, C. "Complementing Cancer Care." *Intensive Journal of Aromatherapy* 3, no. 4 (1991): 15–17.

Irlen, Helen. "Scotocopic Sensitivity Syndrome." *Behavioral Therapy* 2 (January 1992): 77–80.

Keller, W., and W. Kober. "Moglickeiten der Verwendung atherischer ale zur Raudesinfektion I." *Arzeneimittelforschung* 6 (1955): 768.

Levinson, Harold. *Dyslexia: A Solution to the Riddle*. New York: Springer-Verlag, 1980.

Neustaedter, R. "Management of Otitis Media with Effusion in Homeopathic Practice." *Journal of the American Institute of Homeopathy* 79, nos. 3 and 4 (1986).

Price, Shirley. *Aromatherapy for Common Ailments*. New York: Simon and Schuster, 1991.

Schwartz, Ira, and Abe Shapiro, eds., *Collected Works of Lawrence W. Macdonald, volume 2, 1968–1979*. Santa Ana, Calif.: OEP Publishing, 1993.

Shankman, Albert. *Vision Enhancement Training*. Santa Ana, Calif.: OEP Publishing, 1988.

*The Smart Guide to Homeopathy*, pamphlet, Boiron.

Spitler, Harry Riley. *The Syntonic Principle*. Eaton, Ohio: College of Syntonic Optometry Publishing, 1941.

Streff, John. *Stop School Failure*. New York: Harper Row, 1972.

Trachtman, Joseph N. "Learning Problems: Theoretical and Practical Considerations of Information Processing." *Journal of Behavioral Optometry* 11, no. 2 (2000): 35–39.

Woolfson, A. "Intensive Aromacare." *Intensive Journal of Aromatherapy* 4, no. 2 (1992): 12–13.

Zenner, S., and H. Metelmann. "Therapeutic Use of Lymphomyosot— Results of a Multicenter Use Observation Study on 3,512 Patients' Biological Therapy." *Biological Therapy* 8, no. 4 (October 1990): 79.

# Index